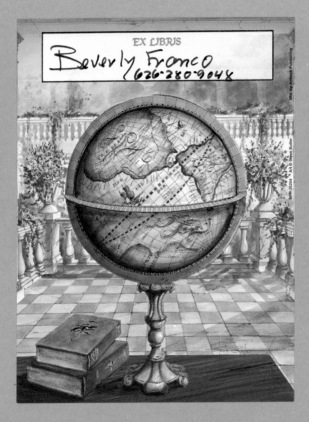

MEDITATIONS ON THE
EARTH

MEDITATIONS ON THE
EARTH

A Celebration of Nature,
in Quotations, Poems, and Essays

COMPILED BY HOLLY HUGHES

ILLUSTRATED BY MARK WEAKLEY

RUNNING PRESS
PHILADELPHIA · LONDON

Canadian representatives: General Publishing Co., Ltd., 30 Lesmill Road,
Don Mills, Ontario M3B 2T6

Excerpt from *Teaching a Stone to Talk* by Annie Dillard copyright © 1982 by
Annie Dillard. Reprinted by permission of HarperCollins Publishers Inc.
and Blanche C. Gregory, Inc.

9 8 7 6 5 4 3 2 1
Digit on the right indicates the number of this printing.

ISBN 1-56138-547-6
Library of Congress Cataloging-in-Publication Number 94-67476

Edited by Gregory C. Aaron
Dust jacket design by Ken Newbaker
Interior design by Jacqueline Spadaro and Ken Newbaker
Dust jacket and interior illustrations by Mark Weakley
Typography: FC Vendôme by Richard Conklin
Printed in the United States

This book may be ordered from the publisher. Please add $2.50
for postage and handling. *But try your bookstore first!*

Running Press Book Publishers
125 South Twenty-second Street

Contents

Introduction

We human beings perceive our surroundings much differently than do our fellow travelers, the animals. Other species seek shelter when rain falls, but humans listen for music in the rhythm of the drops. Other species recognize nightfall as a time to sleep or hunt. As dusk falls, we humans admire the colors of the sunset, imagine that the stars are hung in meaningful designs, and wonder what it would be like to live on the moon. An animal looks at another animal and has two concerns: "Is it good to eat?" and "Will it eat me?" A human being, however, marvels at the way another creature moves, wonders what is going on inside its brain, and often finds that the animal evokes an emotional response.

And so members of the tribe *Homo sapiens* have written, talked, studied, prayed, and philosophized about nature over the centuries. Our prehistoric ancestors daubed paint on cave walls to depict the creatures with which they shared the primeval landscape. The ancient Egyptians, Greeks, and Romans personified natural

phenomena in their gods and goddesses—Ra, Neptune, Iris, Persephone, and a host of others. As fallible and capricious as human beings, these deities acted in myths that sought to explain nature's mysteries.

Medieval Christian and Buddhist monks studied trees, stars, birds, and flowers as a way of knowing the mind of God. During the Renaissance, humanist poets and philosophers turned things on their heads, regarding humans as the pinnacle of creation. If they described animals or landscapes at all, it was generally as a way to illustrate human character and emotion.

By the 18th century, poets were writing precise verse about orderly pastoral scenes, while scientists dissected the universe like clockmakers taking apart an intricate watch. The 19th-century Romantics looked to nature for handy symbols of human imagination, and so they preferred vast, dramatic landscapes—crags, abysses, tangled woods—that expressed the limitless power of the mind.

The natural sciences—biology, botany, geology—rose to importance in the mid-19th century and urged objective, detailed observation of nature. Soon after came the

Golden Age of Nature Writing, as John Muir, John Burroughs, and W. H. Hudson wrote rapturously of their own firsthand experiences in the landscapes they knew best. Explorer-naturalists like Theodore Roosevelt and William Beebe recorded their adventures around the globe, describing exotic locales and species for an appreciative public.

Always the human mind has asked: What is my place in all this? What's my responsibility to this planet? Are other animals here to serve me, or am I here to respect and protect them? Has progress gone too far—or not far enough?

This book brings together many questions and answers. But it's not only an investigation into nature, it's also a celebration of nature, a collection of writers' encounters with nature's endless beauty and variety. Reading what so many other people have seen in their environment, you may find yourself seeing more of the world around you. This is a book to take with you on a morning's bird-watching session or a night of stargazing. Pack it with your picnic on a mountain hike, tote it along for beach reading. Press a

wildflower between its pages, or find a russet-colored autumn leaf for your bookmark. Read, think, and meditate upon nature—after all, it's the human thing to do.

Our Life in Nature

If I were to name the three most precious resources of life, I should say books, friends, and nature; and the greatest of these, at least the most constant and always at hand, is nature. Nature we have always with us, an inexhaustible storehouse of that which moves the heart, appeals to the mind, and fires the imagination,—health to the body, a stimulus to the intellect, and joy to the soul.

John Burroughs (1837–1921)
American writer and naturalist

What nature delivers to us is never stale. Because what nature creates has eternity in it.

Isaac Bashevis Singer (1904–1991)
Polish- born American writer

Perhaps nature is our best assurance of immortality.

Eleanor Roosevelt (1884–1962)
American First Lady and writer

I discovered in nature the nonutilitarian delights that I sought in art. Both were a form of magic, both were a game of intricate enchantment and deception.

Vladimir Nabokov (1899–1977)
Russian poet and novelist

. . . is it politically reprehensible, while we are all groaning, under the shackles of the capitalist system, to point out that life is frequently more worth living because of a blackbird's song, a yellow elm tree in October, or some other natural phenomenon which does not cost money and does not have what the editors of the Left-wing newspapers call a class angle?

George Orwell (1903–1950)
English writer

All nature wears one universal grin.

Henry Fielding (1707–1754)
English novelist and playwright

All my life through, the new sights of Nature made me rejoice like a child.

Marie Curie (1867–1934)
Polish-born French chemist

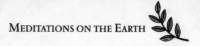

What I love is near at hand,
Always, in earth and sky.

Theodore Roethke (1908–1963)
American poet

Why should we thus, with an untoward mind,
And in the weakness of humanity,
From natural wisdom turn our hearts away;
To natural comfort shut our eyes and ears;
And, feeding on disquiet, thus disturb
The calm of nature with our restless thoughts?

William Wordsworth (1770–1850)
English poet

And I shall have some peace there, for peace comes
    dropping slow,
Dropping from the veils of the morning to where the
    cricket sings;
There midnight's all a glimmer, and noon a purple glow,
And evening full of linnet's wings.

W. B. Yeats (1865–1939)
Irish poet

Our Life in Nature

OUT-OF-DOORS, *n*. That part of one's environment upon which no government has been able to collect taxes. Chiefly useful to inspire poets.

Ambrose Bierce (1842–1914?)
American writer

To him who in the love of Nature holds
Communion with her visible forms, she speaks
A various language.

William Cullen Bryant (1794–1878)
American poet

In her starry shade of dim and
solitary loveliness, I learn the
language of another world.

George Gordon, Lord Byron (1788–1824)
English poet

15

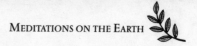

You will find something more in woods than in books.
Trees and stones will teach you that which you can never
learn from masters.

St. Bernard (1091–1153)
French cleric

But ask now the beasts, and they shall teach thee; and the
fowls of the air, and they shall tell thee: Or speak to the
earth, and it shall teach thee: And the fishes of the sea shall
declare unto thee.

Job 12:7–8

Nature is always hinting at us. It hints over and over again.
And suddenly we take the hint.

Robert Frost (1874–1963)
American poet

16

Gie me ae spark o' Nature's fire,
That's a' the learning I desire.

Robert Burns (1759–1796)
Scottish poet

Man must understand his universe in order to understand
his destiny.

Neil Armstrong (b. 1930)
American astronaut

The study of Nature is intercourse with the Highest Mind.
You should never trifle with Nature.

Jean Louis Agassiz (1807–1873)
Swiss naturalist

Great things are done when men and mountains meet;
This is not done by jostling in the street.

William Blake (1757–1827)
English poet and artist

17

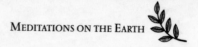

Never does Nature say one thing and wisdom another.

Juvenal (A.D. 50–130)
Roman satirist

Consult Nature in everything and write it all down.
Whoever thinks he can remember the infinite teachings
of Nature flatters himself. Memory is not that huge.

Leonardo da Vinci (1452–1519)
Italian artist and engineer

I have no enthusiasm for nature which the slightest chill
will not instantly destroy.

George Sand (1804–1876)
French novelist

Nature is often hidden, sometimes overcome, seldom
extinguished.

Francis Bacon (1561–1626)
English essayist and philosopher

18

Think of our life in nature,—daily to be shown matter, to come in contact with it,—rocks, trees, wind on our cheeks! the *solid* earth! the *actual* world! the *common sense! contact! Contact! Who* are we? *where* are we?

Henry David Thoreau (1817–1862)
American writer

Hold your hands out over the earth as over a flame. To all who love her, who open to her the doors of their veins, she gives of her strength, sustaining them with her own measureless tremor of dark life. Touch the earth, love the earth, honour the earth, her plains, her valleys, her hills, and her seas; rest your spirit in her solitary places. For the gifts of life are the earth's and they are given to all, and they are the songs of birds at daybreak, Orion and the Bear, and dawn seen over ocean from the beach.

Henry Beston (1888–1968)
American nature writer

Out and About

Whom shall one take with him when he goes a-courting Nature? That is always a vital question. There are persons who will stand between you and that which you seek: they obtrude themselves; they monopolize your attention; they blunt your sense of the shy, half-revealed intelligences about you. I want for companion a dog or a boy, or a person who has the virtues of dogs and boys,— transparency, good-nature, curiosity, open sense, and a nameless quality that is akin to trees and growths and the inarticulate forces of nature.

John Burroughs (1837–1921)
American writer and naturalist

All the world was before me and every day was a holiday, so it did not seem important to which one of the world's wildernesses I first should wander.

John Muir (1838–1914)
Scottish-born American naturalist

 Out and About

Live in the fields, and God will give you lectures on natural philosophy every day. You shall have the snow-bunting, the chickadee, the jay, the partridge, the chrysalis and wasp for your neighbors.

Ralph Waldo Emerson (1803–1882)
American poet and essayist

Inebriate of air am I,
And debauchee of dew,
Reeling, through endless summer days,
From inns of molten blue.

Emily Dickinson (1830–1886)
American poet

I think that I cannot preserve my health and spirits, unless I spend four hours a day at least,—and it is commonly more than that,—sauntering through the woods and over the hills and fields, absolutely free from all worldly engagements.

Henry David Thoreau (1817–1862)
American writer

I nauseate walking; 'tis a country diversion, I loathe
the country.

William Congreve (1670–1729)
English playwright

In those vernal seasons of the year when the air is calm and
pleasant, it were an injury and sullenness against nature
not to go out, and see her riches, and partake in her
rejoicing with heaven and earth.

John Milton (1608–1674)
English poet

There is a pleasure in the pathless woods,
There is a rapture on the lonely shore,
There is society, where none intrudes,
By the deep sea, and music in its roar:
I love not man the less, but Nature more.

George Gordon, Lord Byron (1788–1824)
English poet

And since to look at things in bloom
Fifty springs are little room,
About the woodlands I will go
To see the cherry hung with snow.

A. E. Housman (1859–1936)
English poet

This is what I had come for, just this, and nothing more. A
fling of leafy motion on the cliffs, the assault of real things,
living and still, with shapes and powers under the sky—this
is my city, my culture, and all the world I need.

Annie Dillard (b. 1945)
American writer

And it may have been that his only happy moments were
these at dawn, when he went with his dog over the known
ways, freeing his bronchial tubes of the catarrh that had
oppressed his night, and watching as color gradually
emerged from the indistinct gray among the field rows
and the olive branches, and recognizing the song of the
morning birds one by one.

Italo Calvino (1923–1985)
Italian writer

Go forth, under the open sky, and list
To Nature's teachings.

William Cullen Bryant (1794–1878)
American poet

There is no philosophy with a
shadow of realism about it, save a
philosophy based upon Nature.

Donald Culross Peattie (1898–1964)
American botanist and writer

That I am a saner, healthier, more contented man, with
true standards of life for all my loiterings in the fields and
woods, I am fully convinced.

John Burroughs (1837–1921)
American writer and naturalist

I had a vague feeling of perpetual warm sunny weather,
when I used to be taken driving and notice the speckled
shadows moving across the carriage, before it ocurred to
me that they were caused by the leaves overhead. (As soon
as I discovered this, the scientific interest killed the
impression, and I began speculating as to why the patches
of light were always circular and so on.)

Bertrand Russell (1872–1970)
English mathematician and philosopher

Let us spend one day as deliberately as Nature, and not be
thrown off the track by every nutshell and mosquito's wing
that falls on the rails.

Henry David Thoreau (1817–1862)
American writer

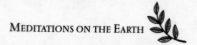

Talk of immortality! After a whole day in the woods, we are already immortal. When is the end of such a day?

John Muir (1838–1914)
Scottish-born American naturalist

In natural objects we feel ourselves, or think of ourselves, only by *likenesses;* among men, too often by *differences.* Hence the soothing, love-kindling effort of rural nature— the bad passions of human societies.

Samuel Taylor Coleridge (1772–1834)
English poet

I have always longed to be a part of the outward life, to be out there at the edge of things, to let the human taint wash away in emptiness and silence . . . to return to the town as a stranger.

J. A. Baker (b. 1926)
English nature writer

26

 Out and About

And forth into the fields I went,
And Nature's living motion lent
The pulse of hope to discontent.

Alfred, Lord Tennyson (1809–1892)
English poet

A nature lover is a person who, when treed by a bear, enjoys
the view.

Anonymous

Letting It In

To see a world in a grain of sand
And a heaven in a wild flower,
Hold infinity in the palm of your hand
And eternity in an hour.

William Blake (1757–1827)
English poet and artist

Even if something is left undone, everyone must take time
to sit still and watch the leaves turn.

Elizabeth Lawrence (b. 1934)
American writer

"Why, one can hear and see the grass growing!" thought
Levin, noticing a wet, slate-colored aspen leaf moving
beside a blade of young grass.

Leo Tolstoy (1828–1910)
Russian writer

Letting It In

. . . Nobody, living upon the remotest, most barren crag in the ocean, could complain of a dull landscape so long as he would lift his eyes. In the sky there was a new landscape every minute, in every pool of the sea rocks, a new world.

T. H. White (1906–1964)
English writer

It is always like this for naturalists, and for poets—the long hours of travel and preparation, and then the longer hours of waiting. All for that one electric, pulse-revving vision when the universe suddenly declares itself.

Diane Ackerman (b. 1948)
American writer

Viewers are as much a part of the landscape as the boulders they stand on.

Leslie Marmon Silko (b. 1948)
American writer

Nature yields nothing to the sybarite. The meadow glows with buttercups in spring, the hedges are green, the wood lovely; but these are not to be enjoyed in their full significance unless you have traversed the same places when bare, and have watched the slow fulfillment of the flowers.

Richard Jefferies (1848–1887)
English writer

No one can write knowingly of weather who walks bent over on wet days.

E. B. White (1899–1985)
American essayist

Being taken by camera into the deepest African jungle, across the Arctic wastes, thirty fathoms deep in the sea, may seem a "miracle of modern technology," but it will no more bring the viewer nearer the reality of nature . . . than merely reading novels is likely to teach the writing of them.

John Fowles (b. 1926)
English writer

30

Like a great poet, Nature is capable of producing the most stunning effects with the smallest means. Nature possesses only the sun, trees, flowers, water and love. But for him who feels no love in his heart, none of these things has any poetic value. To such an individual the sun has a diameter of a certain number of miles, the trees are good for making a fire, the flowers are divided into varieties, and the water is set.

Heinrich Heine (1797–1856)
German poet and critic

Detailed descriptions of landscape are tedious. One part of England is superficially so much like another. The differences are subtle, coloured by love.

J. A. Baker (b. 1926)
English nature writer

Nothing is so tiresome as walking through some beautiful scene with a minute philosopher, a botanist, or a pebble-gatherer, who is eternally calling your attention from the grand features of the natural picture to look at grasses and chuckie-stanes.

Sir Walter Scott (1771–1832)
Scottish poet and novelist

These earthly godfathers of heaven's lights
That give a name to every fixed star
Have no more profit of their shining nights
Than those that walk and wot not what they are.

William Shakespeare (1564–1616)
English playwright and poet

Nature is not a competition. It doesn't really matter, when
you go out, if you don't identify anything. What matters is
the feeling heart.

Richard Adams (b. 1920)
British writer

All through my life I never did believe in human measure-
ment. Numbers, time, inches, feet. All are just ploys for
cutting nature down to size. I know the grand scheme of
the world is beyond our brains to fathom, so I don't try,
just let it in. I don't believe in numbering God's creatures.

Louise Erdrich (b. 1954)
American writer

32

You must not know too much, or be too precise or
scientific about birds and trees and flowers and water
craft; a certain free margin, and even vagueness—perhaps
ignorance, credulity—helps your enjoyment of these
things, and of the sentiment of feathered, wooded, river,
or marine Nature generally. I repeat it—don't want to know
too exactly, or the reasons why.

Walt Whitman (1819–1892)
American poet

These people have learned not from books, but in the
fields, in the wood, on the river bank. Their teachers have
been the birds themselves, when they sang to them, the sun
when it left a glow of crimson behind it at setting, the very
trees, and wild herbs.

Anton Chekhov (1860–1904)
Russian playwright and story writer

It seems to me that we all look at Nature too much, and
live with her too little.

Oscar Wilde (1854–1900)
Irish playwright, poet, and writer

There are dangers in sentimentalizing nature. Most sentimental ideas imply, at bottom, a deep if unacknowledged disrespect. It is no accident that we Americans, probably the world's champions sentimentalizers about nature, are at one and the same time probably the world's most voracious and disrespectful destroyers of wild and rural countryside.

Jane Jacobs (b. 1916)
American social scientist

The field has eyes, the wood has ears; I will look, be silent, and listen.

Hieronymus Bosch (1450?–1516)
Dutch painter

"Bumblebees"

by Walt Whitman (1819–1892)

As a poet, Whitman brought a democratic selection of subject matter to American literature. His interest in all facets of living certainly extended to the natural world. He was an avid hiker and enjoyed a long friendship with nature writer John Burroughs. In this excerpt from Specimen Days *(1882), Whitman displays his characteristic exuberance and sensitivity during a sojourn through the countryside.*

May-month—month of swarming, singing, mating birds—the bumblebee month—month of the flowering lilac (and then my own birth month). As I jot this paragraph, I am out just after sunrise, and down toward the creek. The lights, perfumes, melodies—the bluebirds, grassbirds, and robins, in every direction—the noisy, vocal, natural concert. For undertones, a neighboring woodpecker tapping his tree, and the distant clarion of chanticleer. Then the fresh earth smells—the colors, the delicate drabs and thin blues of the perspective. The bright green of the grass has received an added tinge from the last two days' mildness and moisture. How the sun silently mounts in the broad clear sky, on his day's journey! How the warm beams bathe all, and come streaming kissingly and almost hot on my face.

Later. Nature marches in procession, in sections, like the corps of an army. All have done much for me, and still do. But for the last two days it has been the great wild bee, the humblebee, or "bumble," as the children call him. As I walk, or hobble, from the farmhouse down to the creek, I traverse the before-mentioned lane, fenced by old rails, with many splits, splinters, breaks, holes, etc., the choice habitat of those crooning, hairy insects. Up and down and by and between these rails, they swarm and dart and fly in countless myriads. As I wend slowly along, I am often accompanied with a moving cloud of them. They play a leading part in my morning, mid-day, or sunset rambles, and often dominate the landscape in a way I never before thought of—fill the long lane, not by scores or hundreds only, but by thousands. Large and vivacious and swift, with wonderful momentum and a loud swelling perpetual hum, varied now and then by something almost like a shriek, they dart to and fro, in rapid flashes, chasing each other, and (little things as they are) conveying to me a new and pronounced sense of strength, beauty, vitality, and movement. Are they in their mating season? Or what is the meaning of this plentitude, swiftness, eagerness, display? As I walked, I thought I was followed by a particular swarm, but upon observation I saw that it was a rapid succession of changing swarms, one after another. As I write, I am seated under a big wild cherry tree—the warm day tempered by partial clouds and a fresh breeze, neither too heavy nor light—and here I sit long and long, enveloped in the deep musical drone of these bees, flitting, balancing, darting to and fro about me by hundreds—big fellows with light yellow jackets, great glistening swelling bodies, stumpy heads and gauzy wings—humming their perpetual rich mellow boom. (Is there not a hint in it for a musical composition, of which it should be the background? Some bumblebee symphony?) How it all nourishes, lulls me, in the way most needed; the open air, the rye fields, the apple orchards. The last two days have been faultless in sun, breeze, temperature, and everything; never two more perfect days, and I have enjoyed them wonderfully. My health is somewhat better, and my spirit at peace. . . . Down in the apple trees and in a neighboring cedar were three or four russet-backed thrushes, each singing his best, and roulading in ways I never heard surpassed. Two hours I abandon myself to hearing them, and indolently absorbing the scene. Almost every bird I notice has a special time in the year—sometimes limited to a few days—when it sings its best; and now is the period of these russet-backs. Meanwhile, up and down the lane, the

darting, droning, musical bumblebees. A great swarm again for my entourage as I return home, moving along with me as before. As I write this, two or three weeks later, I am sitting near the brook under a tulip tree, 70 feet high, thick with the fresh verdure of its young maturity—a beautiful object—every branch, every leaf perfect. From top to bottom, seeking the sweet juice in the blossoms, it swarms with myriads of these wild bees, whose loud and steady humming makes an undertone to the whole, and to my mood and the hour.

Using Your Senses

The subtlety of nature is greater many times over than the subtlety of the sense and understanding; so that all those specious meditations, speculations, and glosses in which men indulge are quite from the purpose, only there is no one by to observe it.

Francis Bacon (1561–1626)
English essayist and philosopher

Hold out your hands to feel the luxury of the sunbeams.

Helen Keller (1880–1968)
American writer and lecturer

The grasses become braille as I run my fingers through them.

Terry Tempest Williams (b. 1955)
American nature writer

There is not a single colour hidden away in the chalice of a flower, or the curve of a shell, to which, by some subtle sympathy with the very soul of things, my nature does not answer.

Oscar Wilde (1854–1900)
Irish playwright, poet, and writer

Nay, in some sense, a person who has never seen the rose-color of the rays of dawn crossing a blue mountain twelve or fifteen miles away, can hardly be said to know what *tenderness* in colour means at all . . . .

John Ruskin (1819–1900)
English critic and essayist

The zenith spread its canopy of sapphire, and the West has a magnificent array of clouds, and as the breeze plays on them they assume the forms of mountains, castled cliffs and hills, and shadowy glens, and groves, and beetling rocks, and some in golden masses float, and others have edges of burning crimson.—Never from the birth of time were scattered o'er the glowing sky more splendid colorings.

Noel Thomas Carrington (1777–1830)
English poet

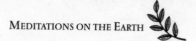

Once it chanced that I stood in the very abutment of a
rainbow's arch, which filled the lower stratum of the
atmosphere, tinging the grass and leaves around, and
dazzling me as if I looked through colored crystal.
It was a lake of rainbow light, in which, for a short while,
I lived like a dolphin.

Henry David Thoreau (1817–1862)
American writer

The lights of the aurora moved and shifted over the horizon. . . . Great streamers of bluish white zigzagged like a

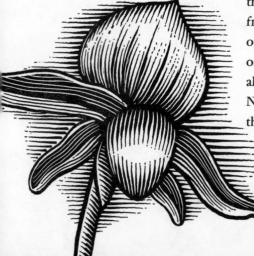

tremendous trembling curtain
from one end of the sky to the
other. Streaks of yellow and
orange and red shimmered
along the flowing borders.
Never for a moment were
they still. . . .

Sigurd Olson (1899–1982)
American teacher and writer

42

 Using Your Senses

The sea is not always blue. . . . In the evening a much more dazzling color may emerge. A wave that feels the bottom, crests and topples will release a phosphorescent surf of pale green or red hue. This glowing, advancing surf can be stunning, like lambent lightening across the sky or a rainbow on the horizon.

Wesley Marx (b. 1934)
American writer and conservationist

Suddenly, as a ship leaves an estuary, we came out on to the steppe: a dazzling open sea of green. I never saw that colour before. In other greens, of emerald, jade, or malachite, the harsh deep green of the Bengal jungle, and sad cool green of Ireland, the salad green of Mediterranean vineyards, the heavy full-blown green of English summer beeches, some element of blue or yellow predominates over the others. This was the pure essence of green, indissoluble, the colour of life itself.

Robert Byron (1905–1941)
English architecture and art critic

It was a warm day. Everything was green, and through the green there was that subtle gold-coming color that makes the green hurt to look at.

James Dickey (b. 1923)
American writer

In the Hall of Gems at the Museum of Natural History in New York, I once stood in front of a huge piece of sulfur so yellow I began to cry. . . . At the time, I called the emotion wonder, and thought: Isn't it extraordinary to be alive on a planet where there are yellows such as this?

Diane Ackerman (b. 1948)
American writer

There is a great restfulness in the sounds these small streams make; they are going down as fast as they can, but their sounds seem leisurely and idle, as if produced like gemstones with the greatest patience and care.

Wendell Berry (b. 1934)
American poet and writer

Only, from the long line of spray
Where the sea meets the moon-blanch'd land,
Listen! you hear the grating roar
Of pebbles which the waves draw back, and fling,
At their return, up the high strand,
Begin, and cease, and then again begin,
With tremulous cadence slow, and bring
The eternal note of sadness in.

Matthew Arnold (1822–1888)
English poet

Listen: a fourworded wavespeech: seesoo, hrss, rsseeiss,
ooos. Vehement breath of waters amid seasnakes, rear-
ing horses, rocks. In cups of rocks it slops: flop, slop,
slap: bounded in barrels. And, spent, its speech ceases.
It flows purling, wisely flowing, floating foampool,
flower unfurling.

James Joyce (1882–1941)
Irish writer

. . . and the sounds of the African night took over—the nightsounds that are always there, thundering away in a kind of subdued bedlam. But the insects' instruments are so subtly orchestrated that you rarely notice them: you filter them out and register only unusual noises. And so, most of the time, you hear only the silence of the night.

Colin Fletcher (b. 1922)
Welsh hiker and writer

The time in our own life when we came closest to being convinced by silence was one time at sea in a light fall of snow. We heard nothing—no gravel, no wind, no waves, no wolves, no bell buoy. It was convincing and it was beautiful.

E. B. White (1899–1985)
American essayist

The sea is a noisy place. Just swim near the parrot fish on a coral reef. You can hear them chewing, *crunch, crunch*. All through the water world, there are grunts, deep moans, snaps, drummings, squeaks, roars, clatters, bangs, and from

time to time through the corridors of water, the calling of the great whales.

Mary Lee Settle (b. 1918)
American writer

I was sitting in a birch wood one autumn, about the middle of September. . . . The leaves scarcely rustled above my head; by their very noise one could know what time of year it was. It was not the happy, laughing *tremolo* of spring, not the soft murmuration and long-winded talkativeness of summer, not the shy and chill babblings of late autumn, but a hardly audible dreamy chattering.

Ivan Turgenev (1818–1883)
Russian writer

The sound of the sea distinctly heard on the tops of the hills, which we could never hear in summer. We attribute this partly to the bareness of the trees, but chiefly to the absence of the singing of birds, the hum of insects, that noiseless noise which lives in the summer air.

Dorothy Wordsworth (1771–1855)
English diarist

How absolute, and omnipotent is the silence of the night! And yet the stillness seems almost audible.—From all the measureless depths of air around us, comes a half sound, a half whisper, as if we could hear the crumbling and falling away of earth and all created things in the great miracle of nature, decay and reproduction ever beginning, never ending—the gradual lapse and running of the sand in the great hourglass of time.

Henry Wadsworth Longfellow (1807–1882)
American poet

I cannot forever keep out the woodpecker that mistakes my house for a dead tree. For that matter, why should I object to a flicker banging away on the roof when what it is doing is proclaiming the triumph of spring?

John Hay (b. 1915)
American nature writer

When one has been long at sea, the smell of land reaches far out to greet one. And the same is true when one has been long inland. I believe I smelled the sea rocks and the kelp and the excitement of churning sea water, the sharpness of iodine and the under odor of washed and ground calcareous shells. Such a far-off and remembered odor comes subtly so that one does not consciously smell it, but rather an electric excitement is released—a kind of boisterous joy.

John Steinbeck (1902–1968)
American writer

Of course, near the shore, he could smell frogs, mud, mussels, rotting fish, muskrats, ducks, cranes, certain snakes, and other shore-hugging creatures; but in the middle of the great Missouri he could smell only whatever happened to be in the boat.

Larry McMurtry (b. 1936)
American writer

Sometimes, however, I go rowing without the rudder. It is fun to try to steer by the scent of watergrasses and lilies, and of bushes that grow on the shore.

Helen Keller (1880–1968)
American writer and lecturer

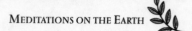

Junipers in the mountains were thickly hung with berries, and the air was unadulterated gin.

John McPhee (b. 1931)
American writer

We others, who have long lost the more subtle of the physical senses, have not even proper terms to express an animal's intercommunications with his surroundings, living or otherwise, and have only the word "smell," for instance, to include the whole range of delicate thrills which murmur in the nose of the animal night and day, summoning, warning, inciting, repelling.

Kenneth Grahame (1859–1932)
English writer

Winds are advertisements of all they touch, however much or little we may be able to read them; telling their wanderings even by their scents alone.

John Muir (1838–1914)
Scottish-born American naturalist

The Eternal Cycles

All is flux, nothing stays still.

Heraclitus (c. 540–c. 480 B.C.)
Greek philosopher

Every moment Nature starts on the longest journey, and
every moment she reaches her goal.

Johann Wolfgang von Goethe (1749–1832)
German poet

The world's a scene of changes, and to be
Constant, in Nature were inconstancy.

Abraham Cowley (1618–1667)
English poet

Nature ever flows; stands never still. Motion or change is
her mode of existence.

Ralph Waldo Emerson (1803–1882)
American poet and essayist

51

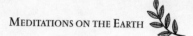

Nature gives to every time and season some beauties of its own; and from morning to night, as from the cradle to the grave, is but a succession of changes so gentle and easy that we can scarcely mark their progress.

Charles Dickens (1812–1870)
English novelist

In nature, there is less death and destruction than death and transmutation.

Edwin Way Teale (1899–1980)
American nature writer

Watching the animals come and go, and feeling the land swell up to meet them and then feeling it grow still at their departure, I came to think of the migrations as breath, as the land breathing. In spring a great inhalation of light and animals. The long-bated breath of summer. And an exhalation that propelled them all south in the fall.

Barry Lopez (b. 1945)
American writer

While the earth remaineth, seedtime and harvest, and cold and heat, and summer and winter, and day and night shall not cease.

Genesis 8:22

The Eternal Cycles

At Christmas I no more desire a rose
Than wish a snow in May's newfangled mirth;
But like of each thing that in season grows.

William Shakespeare (1564–1616)
English playwright and poet

Lo! in the middle of the wood,
The folded leaf is wooed from out the bud
With winds upon the branch, and there
Grows green and broad, and takes no care,
Sun-steeped at noon, and in the moon
Nightly dew-fed; and turning yellow
Falls, and floats adown the air.

Alfred, Lord Tennyson (1809–1892)
English poet

Where are the little yellow aconites of eight weeks ago?
I neither know nor care. They were sunny and the sun
shines, and sunniness means change, and petals passing
and coming.

D. H. Lawrence (1885–1930)
English writer

Birth, life, and death—each took place on the hidden side of a leaf.

Toni Morrison (b. 1931)
American writer

If you stand in a meadow, at the edge of a hillside, and look around carefully, almost everything you can catch sight of is in the process of dying, and most things will be dead long before you are. If it were not for the constant renewal and replacement going on before your eyes, the whole place would turn to stone and sand under your feet.

Lewis Thomas (b. 1913)
American physician and writer

The world thus shaped then is not at rest but eternally revolves with indescribable velocity, each revolution occupying the space of 24 hours: the rising and setting of the sun have left this not doubtful.

Pliny the Elder (23–79 A.D.)
Roman scholar

The sky is round, and I have heard that the earth is round like a ball, and so are all the stars. The wind, in its greatest power, whirls. Birds make their nests in circles, for theirs is the same religion as ours. . . . Even the seasons form a great circle in their changing, and always come back again to where they were.

Black Elk (1863–1950)
Native American (Lakota Sioux) holy man

This grand show is eternal. It is always sunrise somewhere; the dew is never all dried at once; a shower is forever falling; vapor is ever rising. Eternal sunrise, eternal sunset, eternal dawn and gloaming, on sea and continents and islands, each in its turn, as the round earth rolls.

John Muir (1838–1914)
Scottish-born American naturalist

55

A generation goes, and a generation comes,
but the earth remains for ever.
The sun rises and the sun goes down,
and hastens to the place where it rises.
The wind blows to the south,
and goes round to the north;
round and round goes the wind,
and on its circuits the wind returns.
All streams run to the sea,
but the sea is not full;
to the place where the streams flow,
there they flow again.

Ecclesiastes 1:4–7

THE SEASONS

There is no season such delight can bring,
As summer, autumn, winter, and the spring.

William Browne (1591–1674)
English poet

There is a midsummer. There is a midwinter. But there is
no midspring or midautumn. These are the seasons of
constant change.

Edwin Way Teale (1899–1980)
American nature writer

All Nature seems at work. Slugs leave their lair—
The bees are stirring – birds are on the wing—
And Winter slumbering in the open air,
Wears on his smiling face a dream of Spring!

Samuel Taylor Coleridge (1772–1834)
English poet

For lo, the winter is past, the rain is over and gone;
The flowers appear on the earth, and the voice of the turtle
is heard in our land . . . .

The Song of Solomon 2:10–14

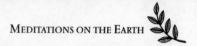

In the spring I have counted one hundred and thirty-six different kinds of weather inside of twenty-four hours.

Mark Twain (Samuel Clemens, 1835–1910)
American humorist and writer

At its best, April is the tenderest of tender salads made crisp by ice or snow water.

John Burroughs (1837–1921)
American writer and naturalist

If spring came but once in a century, instead of once a year, or burst forth with the sound of an earthquake, and not in silence, what wonder and expectation there would be in all hearts to behold the miraculous change! But now the silent succession suggests nothing but necessity. To most men only the cessation of the miracle would be miraculous,

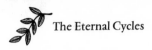

and the perpetual exercise of God's power seems less
wonderful than its withdrawal would be.

Henry Wadsworth Longfellow (1807–1882)
American poet

The pleasures of spring are available to everybody, and
cost nothing.

George Orwell (1903–1950)
English writer

So then the year is repeating its old story again. We are
come once more, thank God! to its most charming chapter.
The violets and the May flowers are as its inscriptions or
vignettes. It always makes a pleasant impression on us,
when we open again at these pages of the book of life.

Johann Wolfgang Von Goethe (1749–1832)
German poet

Every year, back Spring comes, with the nasty little birds
yapping their fool heads off, and the ground all mucked up
with arbutus. Year after year after year.

Dorothy Parker (1893–1967)
American humorist

In the four months since we came here the nights have
warmed, the sea has grown softer, the green, still wintry
water of March has turned in June to blue. . . . There is a
hatching of butterflies, and on the mountain there are
many sweet things for the bees; in the gardens, after a
rainfall, you can faintly, yes, hear the breaking of new
blooms. And we are waking earlier, a sign of summer, and
stay lingering out late in the evening, which is a sign, too.

Truman Capote (1924–1984)
American writer

Today the summer has come at my window
With its sighs and murmurs;
And the bees are plying their minstrelsy
At the court of the flowering grove.

Rabindranath Tagore (1861–1941)
Hindu poet

Summer is the time when one sheds one's tensions with
one's clothes, and the right kind of day is jeweled balm for
the battered spirit. A few of those days and you can become
drunk with the belief that all's right with the world.

Ada Louise Huxtable (b. 1921)
American architecture critic

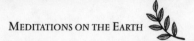

Summer is drawn blinds in Louisiana,
Long winds in Wyoming, shade of elms
and maples in New England.

Archibald MacLeish (1892–1982)
American poet

Do what we can, summer will have its flies; if we walk in the
woods we must feed mosquitos. . . .

Ralph Waldo Emerson (1803–1882)
American poet and essayist

Summer's lease hath all too short a date.

William Shakespeare (1564–1616)
English playwright and poet

The thud of the first apple falling never fails to startle the wits out of me; there has been no sound like it for a year.

May Sarton (b. 1912)
American writer

The leaves in autumn do not change color from the blighting touch of frost, but from the process of natural decay.— They fall when the fruit is ripened, and their work is done.—And their splendid coloring is but their graceful and beautiful surrender of life when they have finished their summer offering of service to God and man.

Tryon Edwards (1809–94)
American theologian

Give me the roughest of spring days rather than the loveliest of autumn days for there is death in the air.

Thomas Hardy (1840–1928)
English novelist and poet

. . . old Autumn in the misty morn standing shadowless like silence listening to silence.

Thomas Hood (1799–1845)
English poet

O wild West Wind, thou breath of Autumn's being,
Thou, from whose unseen presence the leaves dead
Are driven, like ghosts from an enchanter fleeing,
Yellow, and black, and pale, and hectic red,
Pestilence-stricken multitudes . . .

Percy Bysshe Shelley (1792–1822)
English poet

 The Eternal Cycles

Like a fallen woman who sits alone in a dark room
trying not to think of her past, the earth languished with
reminiscence of spring and summer and waited in apathy
for ineluctable winter.

Anton Chekhov (1860–1904)
Russian playwright and story writer

I prefer winter and fall, when you feel the bone structure in
the landscape—the loneliness of it—the dead feeling of
winter. Something waits beneath it—the whole story
doesn't show.

Andrew Wyeth (b. 1917)
American painter

First snow last night . . .
There across the morning bay
Sudden mountain-white.

Shiki (1866–1902)
Japanese poet

Winter is fury—and white silence. It can freeze a blade of grass with a glance. . . . Winter is the jealous season; it demands two distinct years for a single appearance. Mercilessly, it strips the orange and russet from autumn and looks defiantly ahead for spring to step onstage.

Jim Bishop (1907–1987)
American journalist and writer

Perhaps the wind wails so in winter for the summer's dead; and all sad sounds are nature's funeral cries for what has been and is not.

George Eliot (Mary Ann Evans, 1819–1880)
English novelist

The country lay bare and entirely leafless around him, and he thought that he had never seen so far and so intimately into the inside of things as on that winter day when Nature was deep in her annual slumber and seemed to have kicked the clothes off.

Kenneth Grahame (1859–1932)
English writer

 The Eternal Cycles

... a snow-covered plain is the face of death; yet snow is but
the mask of the life-giving rain; it, too, is the friend of
man,—the tender, sculpturesque, immaculate, warming,
fertilizing snow.

John Burroughs (1837–1921)
American writer and naturalist

The last fling of winter is over. . . . The earth, the soil itself
has a dreaming quality about it. It is warm now to the
touch; it has come alive; it hides secrets that in a moment,
in a little while, it will tell.

Donald Culross Peattie (1898–1964)
American naturalist

Therefore all seasons shall be sweet to thee,
Whether the summer clothes the general earth
With greenness, or the redbreast sit and sing
Betwixt the tufts of snow on the bare branch
Of mossy apple-tree, while the nigh thatch
Smokes in the sun-thaw . . . .

William Wordsworth (1770–1850)
English poet

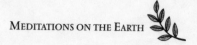

THE HOURS

Rosy-fingered dawn appeared, the early-born.

Homer (c. 700 B.C.)
Greek epic poet

Why does dawn always look like a secret, some shock, sort of an accomplishment? Every sunrise is walled off by the dark, from like company. Maybe each believes it is the very first.

Allan Gurganus (b. 1947)
American writer

Night's candles are burnt out, and jocund day
Stands tiptoe on the misty mountaintops.

William Shakespeare (1564–1616)
English playwright and poet

68

 The Eternal Cycles

The morning dawns with an unwonted crimson; the
flowers more odorous seem; the garden birds sing louder,
and the laughing sun ascends the gaudy earth with an
unusual brightness: all nature smiles, and the whole world
is pleased.

Day Kellogg Lee (1816–1869)
American theologian

The faintness of the stars,
the freshness of the morning,
the dewdrop on the flower,

speaks to me.

Chief Dan George (1899–1981)
Native American (Salish) logger, actor, and poet

And bending across the path as if saying prayers to
welcome the dawn, were long grasses which were
completely overpowered by the thick dew.

Grace Ogot (b. 1930)
Kenyan writer

I was always an early riser. Happy the man who is! Every
morning day comes to him with a virgin's love, full of
bloom and freshness. The youth of nature is contagious,
like the gladness of a happy child.

Edward Bulwer-Lytton (1803–1873)
English novelist and playwright

Sweet is the breath of morn, her rising sweet,
With charm of earliest birds.

John Milton (1608–1674)
English poet

All they could see was sky, water, birds, light, and
confluence. It was the whole morning world.

Eudora Welty (b. 1909)
American writer

'Tis now the hour of deepest noon.
At this still season of repose and peace,
This hour when all things which are not at rest
Are cheerful; while this multitude of flies
With tuneful hum is filling all the air . . .

William Wordsworth (1770–1850)
English poet

70

 The Eternal Cycles

A something in a summer's noon,—
An azure depth, a wordless tune,
Transcending ecstasy.

Emily Dickinson (1830–1886)
American poet

I take a sun bath and listen to the hours, formulating and
disintegrating under the pines, and smell the resiny
hardi-hood of the high noon hours.

Zelda Fitzgerald (1900–1948)
American writer

Then, after the noon-spell, through the long, blazing
evening, (for with us all the time after noon is called
evening) I'd watch the shepherd's hour-glass shutting up
again, and the white clover leaves, folding as the dews
came.

Mary Webb (1881–1927)
English writer

The moon in the sky was a circle of gauze pasted up on the afternoon blue.

Nadine Gordimer (b. 1923)
South African writer

Sometimes in the afternoon sky a white moon would creep up like a little cloud, furtive, without display, suggesting an actress who does not have to "come on" for a while, and so goes "in front" in her ordinary clothes to watch the rest of the company for a moment, but keeps in the background, not wishing to attract attention to herself.

Marcel Proust (1871–1922)
French novelist

Part of the afternoon had waned, but much of it was left, and what was left was of the finest and rarest quality. Real dusk would not arrive for many hours; but the flood of summer light had begun to ebb, the air had grown mellow, the shadows were long upon the dense, smooth turf.

Henry James (1843–1916)
American-born English novelist

Sunsets in themselves are generally superior to sunrises;
and with the sunset we appreciate images drawn from
departed peace, and faded glory.

George Stillman Hillard (1808–1879)
American lawyer and orator

Every sunset which I witness
inspires me with the desire to
go to a West as distant and as
fair as that into which the sun
goes down.

Henry David Thoreau (1817–1862)
American writer

A paler shadow strews its mantle over the mountains;
parting day dies like the dolphin, whom each pang imbues
with a new color as it gasps away, the last still loveliest, till
'tis gone, and all is gray.

George Gordon, Lord Byron (1788–1824)
English poet

More joyful eyes look at the setting, than at the rising
sun.–Burdens are laid down by the poor, whom the sun
consoles more than the rich.–I yearn toward him when he
sets, not when he rises.

Jean Paul Richter (1763–1826)
German humorist

What heart has not acknowledged the influence of this
hour, the sweet and soothing hour of twilight—the hour of
love—the hour of adoration—the hour of rest—when we
think of those we love only to regret that we have not loved
them more dearly; when we remember our enemies only
to forgive them.

Henry Wadsworth Longfellow (1807–1882)
American poet

Dew-drops—nature's tears, which she sheds on her own breast for the fair which die.—The sun insists on gladness; but at night, when he is gone, poor nature loves to weep.

Gamaliel Bailey (1807–59)
American journalist and abolitionist

It was that half-hour after the sunset, the blue half-hour I called it to myself. The wind drops, the light is very beautiful, the mountains sharp, every leaf on every tree is clear and distinct.

Jean Rhys (1890–1979)
Dominican-born English writer

Night is certainly more novel and less profane than day.

Henry David Thoreau (1817–1862)
American writer

What we call "night" is the time we spend facing the secret reaches of space, where other solar systems and, perhaps, other planetarians dwell.

Diane Ackerman (b. 1948)
American writer

NEW LIFE

This I understand: Mother Nature is a maniac. That is to say, she has a mania for reproduction. She maintains life within an organism so long as there is hope of its reproducing itself. Then she kills it off, and does so in the most diverse ways because of her other mania of remaining mysterious.

Italo Svevo (1861–1928)
Italian writer

Along the river, over the hills, in the ground, in the sky, spring work is going on with joyful enthusiasm, new life, new beauty, unfolding, unrolling in glorious exuberant extravagance—new birds in their nests, new winged creatures in the air, and new leaves, new flowers, spreading, shining, rejoicing everywhere.

John Muir (1838–1914)
Scottish-born American naturalist

 The Eternal Cycles

The vegetable life does not content itself with casting from the flower or the tree a single seed, but it fills the air and earth with a prodigality of seeds, that, if thousands perish, thousands may plant themselves; that hundreds may come up, that tens may live to maturity; that at least one may replace the parent.

Ralph Waldo Emerson (1803–1882)
American poet and essayist

A seed hidden in the heart of an apple is an orchard invisible.

Welsh proverb

It was spring here, and juices were getting up in the stalks; leaves, terribly folded in husks, had begun to let loose and open to the light; stuff was stirring in the rot, water bubbled with the froth of sperm and ova, and the whole bog lay rank and eggy, vaporous and thick with the scent of procreation. Things once squeezed close, pinched shut, things waiting to become something else, something greater, were about ready.

William Least Heat Moon (William Trogdon, b. 1939)
American writer

To her children nature seems to have said, "Copulate you must. But beyond that there is no rule. Do it in whatever way and with whatever emotional concomitants you choose. That you should do it somehow or other is all that I ask."

Joseph Wood Krutch (1893–1970)
American writer

The swift is almost continually on the wing; and as it never settles on the ground, on trees, or roofs, would seldom find opportunity for amorous rites, was it not enabled to indulge them in the air.

Gilbert White (1720–1793)
English clergyman

78

And others say, that as *Pearles* are made of glutinous dewdrops, which are condensed by the Suns heat in those Countries, so *Eeles* are bred of a particular dew falling in the moneths of *May* or *June* on the banks of some particular Ponds or Rivers (apted by nature for that end) which in a few dayes is by the Suns heat turned into *Eeles*. . . .

Izaak Walton (1593–1683)
English writer

Big clumsy [may]flies bumped into my face, swarmed on my neck and wiggled in my underwear. Blundering and soft-bellied, they had been born before they had brains. They had spent a year under water on legs, had crawled out on a rock, had become flies and copulated with the ninth and tenth segments of their abdomens, and then had died as the first light wind blew them into the water where the fish circled excitedly.

Norman Maclean (1902–1990)
American writer

Then the great bull [whale] lies up against his bride
in the blue deep of the sea
as mountain pressing on mountain, in the zest of life . . .
in the clasp and the soft, wild clutch of the she-whale's
      fathomless body.

D. H. Lawrence (1885–1930)
English poet and novelist

A male firefly flashes its cool, yellow-green semaphores of
desire, and if the female, too, is randy, she flashes back her
consent. They look hot and bothered, twinkling through a
summer's night like lovers drifting from one streetlamp to
the next.

Diane Ackerman (b. 1948)
American writer

EVOLUTION

There is grandeur in this view of life, with its several
powers, having been originally breathed by the Creator
into a few forms or into one; and that, whilst this planet

has gone cycling on according to the fixed law of gravity, from so simple a beginning endless forms most beautiful and most wonderful have been, and are being evolved.

Charles Darwin (1809–1882)
English naturalist and scientist

Man changes the conditions to suit the things. Nature changes the things to suit the conditions. She adapts the plant or animal to its environment.

John Burroughs (1837–1921)
American writer and naturalist

When, as a very small child, I was playing with a horsetail that had been growing as a weed in one of our flower-beds, dismantling it section by section like a constructional toy, I remember how my father told me it was one of the oldest plants on earth, and I experienced a curious confusion of time. I was holding the oldest plant in my hand, and so I, too, was old.

Jacquetta Hawkes (b. 1910)
English archaeologist and writer

When we go down to the low-tide line, we enter a world that is as old as the earth itself—the primeval meeting place of the elements of earth and water, a place of compromise and conflict and eternal change. For us as living creatures it has special meaning as an area in or near which some entity that could be distinguished as Life first drifted in shallow waters—reproducing, evolving, yielding that endlessly varied stream of living things that has surged through time and space to occupy the earth.

Rachel Carson (1907–1964)
American biologist and writer

There are no short cuts in evolution.

Louis D. Brandeis (1856–1941)
American jurist

It is no accident that mutations occur; the molecule of DNA was ordained from the beginning to make small mistakes.

If we had been doing it, we would have found some way to correct this, and evolution would have been stopped in

its tracks.... Think of the agitated commissions assembled
to explain the scandalous proliferation of trilobites all over
the place, the mass firings, the withdrawal of tenure.

Lewis Thomas (b. 1913)
American biologist and writer

I asserted—and I repeat—that a
man has no reason to be ashamed
of having an ape for his grand-
father. If there were an ancestor
whom I should feel shame in
recalling it would rather be a man
... who ... plunges into scientific
questions with which he has no
real acquaintance....

Thomas Henry Huxley (1825–1895)
English biologist

Is it not possible that mammals look after their young with bumbling consciousness rather than with the expertness of instinct because nature has, in some way, been interested not merely in the survival of the fittest, but in "the fittest" for something more than mere survival?

Joseph Wood Krutch (1893–1970)
American writer

To all the rest, given [Nature] hath sufficient to clad them everyone according to their kind: as namely, shells, cods, hard hides, pricks, shags, bristles, hair, down feathers, quills, scales, and fleeces of wool. The very trunks and stems of trees and plants, she hath defended with bark and rind . . . against the injuries both of heat and cold: man alone, poor wretch, she hath laid all naked upon the bare earth. . . .

Pliny the Elder (A.D. 23–79)
Roman scholar

84

 The Eternal Cycles

Most of the time, you could with advantage look at men as animals—which they are. But you could very rarely look at animals as men—which they are not—and make much sense of it.

Colin Fletcher (b. 1922)
Welsh hiker and writer

The world is fixed, we say: fish in the sea, birds in the air. But in the mangrove swamps by the Niger, fish climb trees and ogle uneasy naturalists who try unsuccessfully to chase them back to the water. There are things still coming ashore.

Loren Eiseley (1907–1977)
American naturalist and writer

"The Four Seasons"

by Henry David Thoreau (1817–1862)

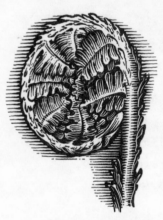

*Three of these evocative passages—
"Spring," "Summer," and "Winter"—are
from Thoreau's* Walden: Or Life in the
Woods *(1854), one of the most celebrated
and imitated works of nature writing, and a
classic of American literature. "Autumn"
is from Thoreau's first book,* A Week on
the Concord and Merrimack Rivers
*(1849), which he wrote during his stay
at Walden Pond.*

"Spring"

At the approach of spring the red-squirrels got under
my house, two at a time, directly under my feet as I sat
reading or writing, and kept up the queerest chuckling and
chirruping and vocal pirouetting and gurgling sounds that
ever were heard; and when I stamped they only chirruped
the louder, as if past all fear and respect in their mad

pranks, defying humanity to stop them. No you don't—chickaree—chickaree. They were wholly deaf to my arguments, or failed to perceive their force, and fell into a strain of invective that was irresistible.

The first sparrow of spring! The year beginning with younger hope than ever! The faint silvery warblings heard over the partially bare and moist fields from the blue-bird, the song-sparrow, and the red-wing, as if the last flakes of winter tinkled as they fell! What at such a time are histories, chronologies, traditions, and all written revelations? The brooks sing carols and glees to the spring. The marsh-hawk sailing low over the meadow is already seeking the first slimy life that awakes. The sinking sound of melting snow is heard in all dells, and the ice dissolves apace in the ponds. The grass flames up on the hillsides like a spring fire,—"*et primitus oritur herba imbribus primoribus evocata,*"—as if the earth sent forth an inward heat to greet the returning sun; not yellow but green is the color of its flame;—the symbol of perpetual youth, the grass-blade, like a long green ribbon, streams from the sod into the summer, checked indeed by the frost, but anon pushing on again, lifting its spear of last year's hay with the fresh life below. It grows as steadily as the rill oozes out of the ground. It is almost identical with that, for in the growing days of June, when the rills are dry, the grass blades are their channels, and from year to year the herds drink at this perennial green stream, and the mower draws from it betimes their winter supply. So our human life but dies down to its root, and still puts forth its green blade to eternity.

"Summer"

Sometimes, in a summer morning, having taken my accustomed bath, I sat in my sunny doorway from sunrise till noon, rapt in a revery, amidst the pines and hickories and sumachs, in undisturbed solitude and stillness, while the birds sang around or flitted noiseless through the house, until by the sun falling in at my west window, or the noise of some traveller's wagon on the distant highway, I was reminded of the lapse of time. I grew in those seasons like corn in the night, and they were far better than any work of the hands would have been. They were not time subtracted from my life, but so much over and above my

usual allowance. I realized what the Orientals mean by contemplation and the forsaking of works. For the most part, I
minded not how the hours went. The day advanced as if to
light some work of mine; it was morning, and lo, now it is
evening, and nothing memorable is accomplished. Instead
of singing like the birds, I silently smiled at my incessant
good fortune. As the sparrow had its trill, sitting on the
hickory before my door, so had I my chuckle or suppressed
warble which he might hear out of my nest. My days were
not days of the week, bearing the stamp of any heathen
deity, nor were they minced into hours and fretted by the
ticking of a clock; for I lived like the Puri
Indians, of whom it is said that "for
yesterday, to-day, and to-morrow they
have only one word, and they express
the variety of meaning by pointing backward for yesterday, forward for to-morrow, and overhead for the passing day."
This was sheer idleness to my fellow-
townsmen, no doubt; but if the birds
and flowers had tried me by their

standard, I should have been found wanting. A man must find his occasions in himself, it is true. The natural day is very calm, and will hardly reprove his indolence.

"Autumn"

As we lay awake long before daybreak, listening to the rippling of the river and the rustling of the leaves, in suspense whether the wind blew up or down the stream, was favorable or unfavorable to our voyage, we already suspected that there was a change in the weather, from a freshness as of autumn in these sounds. The wind in the woods sounded like an incessant waterfall dashing and roaring amid rocks, and we even felt encouraged by the unusual activity of the elements. He who hears the rippling of rivers in these degenerate days will not utterly despair. That night was the turning point in the season. We had gone to bed in summer, and we awoke in autumn; for summer passes into autumn in some unimaginable point of time, like the turning of a leaf.

We found our boat in the dawn just as we had left it, and as if waiting for us, there on the shore, in autumn, all cool and dripping with dew, and our tracks still fresh in the wet sand around it, the fairies all gone or concealed. Before five o'clock we pushed it into the fog, and leaping in, at one shove were out of sight of the shores, and began to sweep downward with the rushing river, keeping a sharp look out for rocks. We could see only the yellow gurgling water, and a solid bank of fog on every side forming a small yard around us. We soon passed the mouth of the Souhegan and the village of Merrimack, and as the mist gradually rolled away, and we were relieved from the trouble of watching for rocks, we saw by the flitting clouds, by the first russet tinge on the hills, by the rushing river, the cottages on shore, and the shore itself, so coolly fresh and shining with dew, and later in the day, by the hue of the grape vine, the goldfinch on the willow, the flickers flying in flocks, and when we passed near enough to the shore, as we fancied, by the faces of men, that the Fall had commenced. . . .

We heard the sigh of the first autumnal wind, and even the water had acquired a grayer hue. The sumach, grape, and maple were already changed, and the milkweed had turned to a deep rich yellow. In all woods the leaves were fast ripening for their fall; for their full veins and lively gloss mark the ripe leaf, and not the sered one of the poets; and we knew that the maples, stripped of their leaves among the earliest, would soon stand like a wreath of smoke along the edge of the meadow. Already the cattle were heard to low wildly in the pastures and along the highways, restlessly running to and fro, as if in apprehension of the withering of the grass and of the approach of winter. Our thoughts too began to rustle.

"Winter"

After a still winter I awoke with the impression that some question had been put to me, which I had been endeavoring in vain to answer in my sleep, as what—how—when—where? But there was dawning Nature, in whom all creatures live, looking in at my broad windows with serene and satisfied face, and no question on *her* lips. I awoke to an answered question, to Nature and daylight. The snow lying deep on the earth dotted with young pines, and the very slope of the hill on which my house is placed, seemed to say, Forward! Nature puts no question and answers none which we mortals ask. She has long ago taken her resolution. "O Prince, our eyes contemplate with admiration and transmit to the soul the wonderful and varied spectacle of this universe. The night veils without doubt a part of this glorious creation; but day comes to reveal to us this great work, which extends from earth even into the plains of the ether."

Then to my morning work. First I take an axe and pail and go in search of water, if that be not a dream. After a

cold and snowy night it needed a divining rod to find it. Every winter the liquid and trembling surface of the pond, which was so sensitive to every breath, and reflected every light and shadow, becomes solid to the depth of a foot or a foot and a half, so that it will support the heaviest teams, and perchance the snow covers it to an equal depth, and it is not to be distinguished from any level field. Like the marmots in the surrounding hills, it closes its eye-lids and becomes dormant for three months or more. Standing on the snow-covered plain, as if in a pasture amid the hills, I cut my way first through a foot of snow, and then a foot of ice, and open a window under my feet, where, kneeling to drink, I look down into the quiet parlor of the fishes, pervaded by a softened light as through a window of ground glass, with its bright sanded floor the same as in summer; there a perennial waveless serenity reigns as in the amber twilight sky, corresponding to the cool and even temperament of the inhabitants. Heaven is under our feet as well as over our heads.

Nature's Laws

The chess board is the world, the pieces are the
phenomena of the universe, the rules of the game
are what we call the laws of Nature. The player on the
other side is hidden from us. We know that his play is
always fair, just, and patient. But also we know, to our cost,
that he never overlooks a mistake, or makes the smallest
allowance for ignorance.

Thomas Henry Huxley (1825–1895)
English biologist

Everything in nature acts in conformity with law.

Immanuel Kant (1724–1804)
German philosopher

Nature is an endless combination and repetition of a
very few laws. She hums the old well-known air through
innumerable variations.

Ralph Waldo Emerson (1803–1882)
American essayist and poet

Nature does nothing uselessly.

Aristotle (384–322 B.C.)
Greek philosopher

Nature's rules have no exceptions.

Herbert Spencer (1820–1903)
English philosopher

It is far from easy to determine whether [Nature] has
proved to man a kind parent or a merciless stepmother.

Pliny the Elder (23–79 A.D.)
Roman scholar

It is interesting to contemplate a tangled bank, clothed
with many plants of many kinds, with birds singing on the
bushes, with various insects flitting about, and with worms
crawling through the damp earth, and to reflect that these
elaborately constructed forms, so different from each
other, and dependent upon each other in so complex a
manner, have all been produced by laws acting around us.

Charles Darwin (1809–1882)
English naturalist and scientist

 Nature's Laws

Laws of Nature are God's thoughts thinking themselves
out in the orbits and the tides.

Charles Henry Parkhurst (1842–1933)
American clergyman

I shall never believe that God plays dice with the world.

Albert Einstein (1879–1955)
German-born American physicist

God not only plays dice with the universe, but sometimes
throws them where we can't see them.

Stephen Hawking (b. 1942)
English physicist

Monotony is the law of nature. Look at the monotonous
manner in which the sun rises.

Mahatma Gandhi (1869–1948)
Indian political leader

Nature does not proceed by leaps.

Carolus Linnaeus (1707–1778)
Swedish botanist

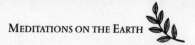

In nature there are neither rewards nor punishments—
there are consequences.

R. D. Ingersoll (1833–1899)
American attorney

Nature is an instructed and impartial teacher, spreading no
crude opinions, and flattering none; she will be neither
radical nor conservative.

Henry David Thoreau (1817–1862)
American writer

The perpetuation of my matter in crocus, coal, or comet is
all I need know about the next act—that atoms continue
in nature.

Robert Michael Pyle (b. 1947)
American nature writer

Constituted as we are it is easier to conceive how the slime floating upon the waters might become in time Homo sapiens than it is to imagine how so complex a thing as a crystal could have been and can always remain just what it is – complicated and perfect but without any meaning, even for itself. How can the lifeless even obey a law?

Joseph Wood Krutch (1893–1970)
American writer

Nature's laws affirm instead of prohibit. If you violate her laws you are your own prosecuting attorney, judge, jury, and hangman.

Luther Burbank (1849–1926)
American horticulturalist

The spider on its web was an engineer who spanned his delicate reaches in terms of a discipline and order that were beyond my grasp.

Johy Hay (b. 1915)
American nature writer

99

Survival

Now where there are seeds and insects there will be birds and small mammals and where these are, will come the slinking, sharp-toothed kind that prey on them.

Mary Austin (1868–1934)
American writer

I am astonished to see that nothing exists but what has its enemy; one species pursues and lives upon the other . . .

Hector St. John de Crèvecoeur (1735–1813)
French-born American farmer and writer

If it is part of the economy of nature for one animal to prey upon some other beneath it, then the poor devil has indeed a mouthful that makes a meal off the porcupine.

John Burroughs (1837–1921)
American writer and naturalist

Survival

So, naturalists observe, a flea
Hath smaller fleas that on him prey;
And these have smaller still to bite 'em;
And so proceed *ad infinitum*.

Jonathan Swift (1667–1745)
Irish cleric and writer

We have unmistakable proof that throughout all past
time, there has been a ceaseless devouring of the weak by
the strong.

Herbert Spencer (1820–1903)
English philosopher

Nature teaches beasts to know their friends.

William Shakespeare (1564–1616)
English playwright and poet

101

Hitherto I had stuck to my resolution of not eating animal food, and on this occasion I consider'd, with my master Tryon, the taking every fish as a kind of unprovok'd murder. . . . But I had formerly been a great lover of fish, and, when this came hot out of the frying-pan, it smelt admirably well. I balanc'd some time between principal and inclination, till I recollected that, when the fish were opened, I saw smaller fish taken out of their stomachs; then thought I, "if you eat one another, I don't see why we mayn't eat you." So I din'd upon cod very heartily. . . .

Benjamin Franklin (1706–1790)
American statesman, printer, inventor

Now this is the Law of the Jungle—as old and as true as
    the sky;
And the Wolf that shall keep it may prosper, but the Wolf
    that shall break it must die.

Survival

As the creeper that girdles the tree-trunk the Law runneth
    forward and back—
For the strength of the Pack is the Wolf, and the strength of
    the Wolf is the Pack.

Rudyard Kipling (1865–1936)
English writer

I do not like opossums to
hustle their dinners in my
chicken coop or beehives,
but that is the way creatures
get on, and I would not kill
one for doing so, Ozark
custom to the contrary.

Sue Hubbell (b. 1935)
American beekeeper and writer

We behold the face of nature bright with gladness, we often see superabundance of food; we do not see or we forget, that the birds which are idly singing round us mostly live on insects or seeds, and are thus constantly destroying life; or we forget how largely these songsters, or their eggs, or their nestlings, are destroyed by birds and beasts of prey; we do not always bear in mind, that, though food may not be superabundant, it is not so at all seasons of each recurring year.

Charles Darwin (1809–1882)
English naturalist and scientist

It was when I began to find out the ways of wasps with other insects on which they nourish their young that my pleasure in them became mixed with pain. . . . Thus the old vexed question—How to reconcile these facts with the idea of a beneficent Being who designed it all—did not come to me from reading, nor from teachers, since I had none, but was thrust upon me by nature itself.

W. H. Hudson (1841–1922)
Argentine-born English naturalist and writer

104

Survival

I appreciate possums in the same way I admire starlings
and cabbage butterflies and reed canary grass—not as
native species, but as tough, clever, evolutionarily and
ecologically astute organisms – as survivors, against
all we dish out.

Robert Michael Pyle (b. 1947)
American nature writer

The awe one feels in an encounter with a polar bear is, in
part, simple admiration for the mechanisms of survival it
routinely employs to go on living in an environment that
would defeat us in a few days.

Barry Lopez (b. 1945)
American writer

Each ant, each lizard, each lark [in the desert] is imbued
with great value simply because the creature is there,
simply because the creature is alive in a place where any
life at all is precious.

Leslie Marmon Silko (b. 1948)
American writer

105

Anything that lives where it would seem that nothing could live, enduring extremes of heat and cold, sunlight and storm, parching aridity and sudden cloudbursts . . . any such creature, beast, bird, or flower, testifies to the grandeur and heroism inherent in all forms of life. Including the human. Even in us.

Edward Abbey (1927–1989)
American writer

The Living Planet

As for the earth, out of it comes bread; but underneath it is
   turned up as by fire.
Its stones are the place of sapphires, and it has dust of gold.

Job 28: 5–6

Ever since life appeared on earth it has been influencing
the history of the earth's crust: shellfish live and die,
live and die, and in time their empty shells build the
[canyon wall]; a tree root pries open a fissure, and in time
another rock falls. But these have been slow, random,
undirected influences.

Colin Fletcher (b. 1922)
Welsh hiker and writer

Geologists on the whole are inconsistent drivers. When a
roadcut presents itself, they tend to lurch and weave. To
them, the roadcut is a portal, a fragment of a regional story,
a proscenium arch that leads their imaginations into the
earth and through the surrounding terrain.

John McPhee (b. 1931)
American writer

... but there was no mud like what they found in Minnesota. The town sat in a swamp from April until June, and then again in July, and often in August, too, while September brought some more, and one October, three days of rain made them a lake that promptly froze over for six months, a spacious icecap, though that was an unusually cold winter—often, January brought a false thaw and a week or two of mud.

Garrison Keillor (b. 1942)
American humorist

Every stone is nothing else but a congealed lump of frozen earth.

Plutarch (46–120 A.D.)
Greek biographer and moralist

The world is the geologist's great puzzle box.

Louis Agassiz (1807–1873)
American naturalist

A rock has being or spirit, although we may not understand it.

Leslie Marmon Silko (b. 1948)
Native American (Pueblo) writer

A bad earthquake at once destroys our oldest associations:
the earth, the very emblem of solidity, had moved beneath
our feet like a thin crust over a fluid;—one second of
time has created in the mind a strange idea of insecurity,
which hours of reflection would not have produced.

Charles Darwin (1809–1882)
English naturalist and scientist

This backbone of Manhattan, into the heart of which the
stolid workmen guide their quivering drills, was formed
in the very dawn of the world: 2,000,000,000 years is a
conservative estimate of its age. Look at it as it crops out
here and there in Central Park—quiet, gray, patient—and
our individual worries will seem of less importance.

William Beebe (1877–1962)
American naturalist and explorer

109

Weather Report

Sunshine is delicious, rain is refreshing, wind braces us up, snow is exhilarating; there's really no such thing as bad weather, only different kinds of good weather.

John Ruskin (1814–1900)
English art critic and writer

Being great as the president is not a matter of knowledge, or farsightedness. It's just a question of the weather—not only in your own country, but in a dozen others. It's the elements that make you great, or break you.

Will Rogers (1879–1935)
American humorist

"... It's a great thing to ha' studied the look o' the clouds. Lord bless you! Th' met'orological almanecks can learn me nothing, but there's a pretty sight o' things I could let *them* up to, if they'd just come to me."

George Eliot (Mary Ann Evans, 1819–1880)
English novelist

 Weather Report

This is Methodist weather—sprinkling. We Baptists prefer total immersion.

Adam Clayton Powell Jr. (1908–1972)
American clergyman and politician

How beautiful is the rain!
After the dust and heat,
In the broad and fiery street,
And in the narrow lane;
How beautiful is the rain!

Henry Wadsworth Longfellow (1807–1882)
American poet

It will talk as long as it wants, this rain.
As long as it talks I am going to listen.

Thomas Merton (1915–1968)
American writer and Trappist monk

At all times I love rain, the early momentous
thunderdrops, the perpendicular cataract shining,
or at night the little showers, the spongy mists, the
tempestuous mountain rain.

Edward Thomas (1878–1917)
English poet and nature writer

Week after week, month after month, the sun looked down
from the cloudless sky, till the karroo bushes were leafless
sticks, broken into the earth, and the earth itself was naked
and bare; and only the milk-bushes, like old hags, pointed
their shrivelled fingers heavenwards, praying for the rain
that never came.

Olive Schreiner (1855–1920)
South African writer and feminist

There is one thing they do not have in England that we can
boast of at home, and that is a good masculine type of
weather: it is not even feminine; it is childish and puerile,
though I am told that occasionally there is a full-grown

storm. But I saw nothing but petulant little showers and prolonged juvenile sulks. The clouds have no reserve, no dignity; if there is a drop of water in them (and there generally are several drops), out it comes.

John Burroughs (1837–1921)
American writer and naturalist

Think of the storm roaming the sky uneasily
like a dog looking for a place to sleep in,
listen to it growling.

Elizabeth Bishop (1911–1979)
American poet

Thunder is the voice of God, and, therefore, to be dreaded.

Increase Mather (1639–1723)
American clergyman, writer, college president

Thunder is good, thunder is impressive; but it is lightning that does the work.

Mark Twain (Samuel Clemens, 1835–1910)
American humorist and writer

113

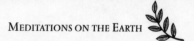

Thunder does all the barking,
but it's lightning that bites.

Young child, quoted by
Art Linkletter (b. 1912)
American TV personality

Lightning seems to have lost its menace. Compared to
what is going on on earth today, heaven's firebrands are
penny fireworks with wet fuses.

E. B. White (1899–1985)
American essayist

It ain't a fit night out for man or beast.

W. C. Fields (1879–1946)
American actor

114

After the wet dark days, the country seems more populous.
It peoples itself in the sunbeams.

Dorothy Wordsworth (1771–1855)
English diarist

Full many a glorious morning have I seen
Flatter the mountaintops with sovereign eye,
Kissing with golden face the meadows green,
Gilding pale streams with heavenly alchemy.

William Shakespeare (1564–1616)
English playwright and poet

But mighty nature bounds as from her birth:
The sun is in the heavens, and life on earth;
Flowers in the valley, splendor in the beam,
Health in the gale, and freshness in the stream.

George Gordon, Lord Byron (1788–1824)
English poet

115

Thank heavens, the sun has gone in, and I don't have to go out and enjoy it.

Logan Pearsall Smith (1865–1946)
American-born English essayist

Weather forecast for tonight: dark.

George Carlin (b. 1938)
American comedian

I have always maintained that if you looked closely enough you could *see* the wind—the dim, hardly-made-out, fine débris fleeing high in the air.

Stewart Edward White (1873–1946)
American writer

In the skin of our fingers we can see the trail of the wind; it shows us where the wind blew when our ancestors were created.

Navajo legend

 Weather Report

Books on nature seldom mention wind; they are written behind stoves.

Aldo Leopold (1888–1948)
American conservationist and writer

The wind shows us how close to the edge we are.

Joan Didion (b. 1934)
American writer

Wind . . . is a cloth that sails so birds have something to fly on.

Gretel Ehrlich (b. 1946)
American writer and rancher

How gently the winds blow! Scarce can these tranquil air currents be called winds. They seem the very breath of Nature, whispering peace to every living thing.

John Muir (1838–1914)
Scottish-born American naturalist

Way out here they have a name for wind, the wind they call
Maria. They could, more sensibly, call it a son-of-a-bitch.

William Least Heat Moon (William Trogdon, b. 1939)
American writer

Although I know it is wrong to curse the wind, I do
it anyway.

Richard K. Nelson (b. 1941)
American anthropologist

. . . ye breezes and soft airs,
Whose subtle intercourse with breathing flowers,
Feelingly watched, might teach Man's haughty race
How without injury to take, to give
Without offense; ye who, as if to show
The wondrous influence of power gently used,
Bend the complying heads of lordly pines,
And, with a touch, shift the stupendous clouds
Through the whole compass of the sky. . .

William Wordsworth (1770–1850)
English poet

The fog comes
on little cat feet.

Carl Sandburg (1878–1967)
American poet

The frost performs its secret ministry
Unhelped by any wind.

Samuel Taylor Coleridge (1772–1834)
English poet

We get a little snow, then a few inches, then another inch or
two, and sometimes we get a ton. The official snow gauge is
a Sherwin-Williams paint can stuck to the table behind the
town garage, with the famous Sherwin-Williams globe and
red paint spilling over the Arctic icecap. When snow is up
to the top of the world, then there is a ton of snow.

Garrison Keillor (b. 1942)
American humorist

Down came the dry flakes, fat enough and heavy enough to crash like nickels on stone. It always surprised him, how quiet it was. Not like rain, but like a secret.

Toni Morrison (b. 1931)
American writer

From my stationary position the most reasonable explanation [for the snowstorm] seemed to be simply that winter had not quite liked the looks of the landscape as she first made it up. She was changing the sheets.

Joseph Wood Krutch (1893–1970)
American writer

A lot of people like snow. I find it to be an unnecessary freezing of water.

Carl Reiner (b. 1922)
American film director and humorist

It was so cold I almost got married.

Shelley Winters (b. 1922)
American actress

"I shouldn't be surprised if it hailed a good deal
tomorrow," Eeyore was saying. "Blizzards and whatnot.
Being fine today doesn't Mean Anything. It has no
sig—what's that word? Well, it has none of that.
It's just a small piece of weather."

A. A. Milne (1882–1956)
English poet and writer

I've lived in good climate, and it bores the hell out of me.
I like weather rather than climate.

John Steinbeck (1902–1968)
American writer

The Continents

The lands [of the planet] wait for those who can discern
their rhythms.

Vine Victor Deloria, Jr. (b. 1933)
Native American (Sioux) writer

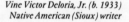

AFRICA

The air in Africa is more significant in the landscape than
in Europe, it is filled with loomings and mirages, and is in a
way the real stage of activities. In the heat of the midday
the air oscillates and vibrates like the string of a violin, lifts
up long layers of grass-land with thorn-trees and hills on it,
and creates vast silvery expanses of water in the dry grass.

Isak Dinesen (Karen Blixen, 1885–1962)
Danish writer

. . . I felt overwhelmed by the age and might of this old
continent, and drained of strength: all seemed pointless in
such emptiness, there was nowhere to go. I wanted to lie

 The Continents

flat out on my back on this almighty mud, but instead I returned slowly into Kenya, pursued by the mutter of primordial birds.

Peter Matthiessen (b. 1927)
American writer

Like clouds, the savannah bush formed and re-formed under the changes of light, moved or gave the impression of being moved past by the travelling eye; silent and ashy green as mould spread and always spreading, rolling out under the sky before her.

Nadine Gordimer (b. 1923)
South African writer

Africa had the last say, and it had it in the form of rats and ants, of the forest swallowing up the little pits the Dutch prospectors had made and abandoned.

Graham Greene (1904–1991)
English writer

Africa has always walked in my mind proudly upright, an African giant among the other continents, toes well dug into the final ocean of one hemisphere, rising to its full height in the graying skies of the other; head and shoulders broad, square and enduring, making light of the bagful of blue Mediterranean slung over its back as it marches patiently through time.

Laurens Van Der Post (b. 1906)
South African writer

The Continents

ANTARCTICA

In many ways, the Antarctic is a world of suspended animation. Suspended between outer space and the fertile continents. Suspended in time—without a local civilization to make history.

Diane Ackerman (b. 1948)
American writer

ASIA

These were free-ranging, expansive, well-watered grassy meadowlands with a host of small pastures, miniature lakes, streams and large ponds overgrown at each end with willows, absolutely Russian, places dear to the heart of the Russian people, like the places to which the legendary warriors of our old folk sagas used to travel to shoot white swans and grey-hued ducks.

Ivan Turgenev (1818–1883)
Russian writer

The brown-green, sunburned hills, the lilac distance with its tints as restful as shade, the plain with its misty limits, and the inverted-looking sky—for in the steppes, where there are no forests or high mountains, the sky seems fearfully deep and pellucid—at this moment appeared limitless and torpid with grief.

Anton Chekhov (1860–1904)
Russian playwright and story writer

Except for the gray eagle and an occasional far-seen bear grubbing and rooting on the [Tibetan] hillside, the vision of a furious painted leopard met at dawn in a still valley devouring a goat, and now and again a bright-coloured bird, they were alone with the winds and the grass singing under the wind.

Rudyard Kipling (1865—1936)
English writer

And at the end [of our journey] I would meet my old love, the Himalayas. We would climb up into their airy heights and complete our journey amongst the icefields from which [the river] Ganga draws its first drops of water.

Sir Edmund Hillary (b. 1919)
New Zealand mountaineer

The cherries in the Heian Shrine were left to the last
because they, of all the cherries in Kyoto, were the most
beautiful . . . . picking the moment of regret when the
spring sun was about to set, they would pause, a little tired,
under the trailing branches, and look fondly at each tree—
on around the lake, by the approach to a bridge, by a bend
in the path, under the eaves of the gallery. And, until the
cherries came the following year, they could close their
eyes and see again the color and line of a trailing branch.

Junichiro Tanizaki (1886–1965)
Japanese novelist

AUSTRALIA

. . . in [Australia,] that silent lost land of the South.
Where nothing bites but insects and snakes and the sun,
　　small life.
Where no bull roared, no cow ever lowed, no stag cried, no
　　leopard screeched, no lion coughed, no dog barked.
But all was silent save for parrots occasionally, in the
　　haunted blue bush.

D. H. Lawrence (1885–1930)
English poet and novelist

127

It is only now and then, in a jungle, or amidst the towering white menace of a burnt or burning Australian forest, that Nature strips the moral veils from vegetation and we apprehend its stark ferocity.

H. G. Wells (1866–1946)
English writer

EUROPE

In winter nothing more dreary, in summer nothing more divine, than those glens shut in by hills, and those bluff, bold swells of heath.

Emily Brontë (1818–1848)
English poet and novelist, on her native Yorkshire moors

It was beautiful here in these wintry heights: not mildly and ingratiatingly beautiful, more as the North Sea is beautiful in a westerly gale. . . . He took his skis and went up on the funicular to the Schatzalp; there, rapt six thousand feet above the sea, he revelled at will on the gleaming slopes of powdery snow—whence, in good weather, there was a view of majestic extent over all the surrounding territory.

Thomas Mann (1876–1955)
German writer

 The Continents

So this is the Riviera! It was bare, as they edged along the
sea. Scrub pine and oak clung to the towering gray rocks to
the north. Now they would be running close by the sea
with jagged gray promontories catching the low surges,
then . . . they would see the low coastal range, the *Alpes
Maritimes,* rugged, bare eminences of stratified gray rock,
treeless for the most part. . . . A curious bare country
into which the sun beat all day long.

William Carlos Williams (1883–1963)
American poet

. . .there among the tamarisks and scattered cork trees appeared the real Sicily
again . . . aridly undulating to the horizon
in hillock after hillock, comfortless and
irrational, with no lines that the mind
could grasp, conceived apparently in a
delirious moment of creation; a sea
suddenly petrified at the instant when
a change of wind had flung waves
into frenzy.

Giuseppe di Lampedusa (1896–1957)
Italian aristocrat and writer

The other thing I long for with you—which we can get sooner—is the Atlantic—the Connemara coast—driving mist-rain—waves that moan on the rocks—flocks of seabirds with wild notes that seem the very soul of the restless sadness of the sea—and gleams of sun, unreal, like glimpses into another world—and wild wild wind, free and strong and fierce—There, there is life. . . .

Bertrand Russell (1872–1970)
English mathematician and philosopher

NORTH AMERICA

The United States: really a quartering of a continent, a drawer in North America. Pull it out and prairie dogs would spill off one side, alligators off the other . . . .

John McPhee (b. 1931)
American writer

. . . for a transitory enchanted moment man must have held his breath in the presence of this continent, compelled

 The Continents

into an aesthetic contemplation he neither understood
nor desired, face to face for the last time in history with
something commensurate to his capacity for wonder.

F. Scott Fitzgerald (1896–1940)
American novelist

SOUTH AMERICA

. . . as we drove through the [Patagonian] desert, I sleepily
watched the rags of silver cloud spinning across the sky,
and the sea of grey-green thornscrub lying off in sweeps
and rising in terraces and the white dust streaming off the
saltpans, and, on the horizon, land and sky dissolving into
an absence of color.

Bruce Chatwin (1942–1989)
English travel writer

Landscapes

We are the children of our landscape. . . .

Lawrence George Durrell (1912–1990)
British poet

THE HORIZON

In every landscape the point of astonishment is the
meeting of the sky and the earth, and that is seen from
the first hillock as well as from the top of the Alleghenies.

Ralph Waldo Emerson (1803–1882)
American poet and essayist

The calmness, the solitude of horizons lures me towards
them, through them, and on to others.

J. A. Baker (b. 1926)
English nature writer

 Landscapes

Elsewhere the sky is the roof of the world; but here the
earth was the floor of the sky.

Willa Cather (1876–1947)
American novelist

THE DESERT

There's something about the desert that doesn't like man,
something that mocks his nesting instinct and makes his
constructions look feeble and temporary. Yet it's just that
inhospitableness that endears the arid rockiness, the places
pointy and poisonous, to men looking for its discipline.

William Least Heat Moon (William Trogdon, b. 1939)
American writer

It is a lovely and terrible wilderness, such a wilderness
as Christ and the prophets went out into; harshly and
beautifully colored, broken and worn until its bones are
exposed, its great sky without a smudge or taint from
Technocracy, and in hidden corners and pockets under its
cliffs the sudden poetry of springs.

Wallace Stegner (1909–1993)
American writer

For all the toll the desert takes of a man it gives
compensation, deep breaths, deep sleep, and the
communion of the stars.

Mary Austin (1868—1934)
American writer

Night comes to the desert all at once, as if someone turned
off the light.

Joyce Carol Oates (b. 1938)
American writer

And if I had not been able periodically to renew myself in
the mountains and deserts of western America I would be
very nearly bughouse.

Wallace Stegner (1909–1993)
American writer

 Landscapes

After the reconnoitering dust-devils comes the real, the
serious wind, the voice of the desert rising to a demented
howl and blotting out sky and sun behind yellow clouds of
dust, sand, confusion, embattled birds, last year's scrub-
oak leaves, pollen, the husks of locusts, bark of juniper . . . .

Edward Abbey (1927–1989)
American writer

The desert is unpredictable, enigmatic. One minute you
will be smelling dust. The next, the desert can smell just
like rain.

Gary Paul Nabhan (b. 1952)
American ethnobiologist

It is asserted as a well-known fact that this desert is the
abode of many evil spirits, which amuse travellers to their
destruction with most extraordinary illusions.

Marco Polo (1254–1324)
Italian merchant and traveler

The desert at night is a great open-air dome, the largest bedchamber in the world.

Carlos Fuentes (b. 1928)
Mexican writer

Stand on the mesa edge . . . so little lies between you and the sky. So little lies between you and the earth. One look and you know that simply to survive is a great triumph, that every possible resource is needed, every possible ally — even the most humble insect or reptile.

Leslie Marmon Silko (b. 1948)
Native American (Pueblo) writer

To enter the Sahara is like passing into a vast chamber that earth has surreptitiously held in trust. Instinctively one moves as in a cathedral — with respect and constant awe . . . even at high noon the Sahara is quieter than any midnight elsewhere.

Noel Mostert (b. 1929)
South African-born American writer

136

 Landscapes

The desert landscape is always at its best in the half-light of dawn or dusk. The sense of distance lacks: a ridge nearby can be a far-off mountain range, each small detail can take on the importance of a major variant on the countryside's repetitious theme. The coming of day promises a change; it is only when the day has fully arrived that the watcher suspects it is the same day returned once again — the same day he has been living for a long time, over and over, still blindingly bright and untarnished by time.

Paul Bowles (b. 1910)
American writer

The problem today is that there are no deserts, only dude ranches.

Thomas Merton (1915–1968)
American writer and Trappist monk

Desert is where I want to be when there are no more questions asked.

Ann Haymond Zwinger (b. 1925)
American nature artist and writer

THE MOUNTAINS

To see the greatness of a mountain, one must keep
one's distance . . . .

Anagarika Brahmacari Govinda (b. 1898)
German-born Buddhist priest

Regions mountainous and wild, thinly inhabited, and little
cultivated, make a great part of the earth, and he that has
never seen them, must live unacquainted with much of
the face of nature, and with one of the great scenes of
human existence.

Samuel Johnson (1709–1784)
English critic, poet, and essayist

Mountains are earth's undecaying monuments.

Nathaniel Hawthorne (1804–1864)
American writer

With what immeasurable patience, what infinite
deliberation, has nature amassed the materials for
these mountains!

Clarence King (1842–1901)
American geologist and writer

 Landscapes

Pouring floods of rain. . .
Won't Mount Fuji wash away
To a muddy lake?

Buson (1715–1783)
Japanese poet

. . . [Mount] Etna herself appeared to approve because
once, just to show me that the world was rightside up, she
spat out a mouthful of hot coals, and then dribbled a small
string of blazing diamonds down her chin.

Lawrence Durrell (1912–1990)
Indian-born British writer

Yet it is a singular contradiction that in their outlines old
mountains look young, and young mountains look old. . . .
All the gauntness, leanness, angularity, and crumbling
decrepitude are with the young mountains; all the
smoothness, plumpness, graceful, flowing lines of youth
are with the old mountains.

John Burroughs (1837–1921)
American writer and naturalist

There is a perfect freedom in the mountains, but it belongs to the eagle and the elk, the badger and the bear.

N. Scott Momaday (b. 1934)
American writer

All around were fine mountain peaks. . . . No wonder, I thought, that the people of the plains have their gods live here; no wonder, too, that anyone seeking the world of the spirit should travel here to find it amidst the mysteries of snow, mountains, sky, and clouds and high pastures.

Sir Edmund Hillary (b. 1919)
New Zealand mountaineer

We may have experienced the most ghastly horrors of bursting shell or crashing bomb, but all fades into fire-cracker comedy when once we have stood on the rim of an active volcano, and watched the lava blood-stream of Mother Earth.

William Beebe (1877–1962)
American naturalist and explorer

THE JUNGLE

The rain forest is perhaps
more truly a silent world
than the sea. The wind
scarcely penetrates; it is not
only silent, it is still. All
sound then gains a curiously
enhanced mystery. A sudden
crack — what could have
made it? An inexplicable
gurgle. . . . A whistle,
impossible to identify
But mostly silence.

Marston Bates (1906–1974)
American biologist

For me the rain forest is the greatest of fantasy lands, a
place of hope still unchained by exact knowledge.

Edward O. Wilson (b. 1929)
American entomologist

I had always pictured jungle as suffocating spaghetti tangles . . . a wicked salad that stank in your face and flung its stalks around you.

This was more like a church, with pillars and fans. . . . There was nothing smothering about it, and although it was noisy with birds, it was motionless — no wind, not even a breeze in the moisture and green shadows and blue-brown trunks. And no tangles — only a forest of verticals, hugely patient and protective.

Paul Theroux (b. 1941)
American writer

Here Nature is unapproachable with her green, airy canopy, a sun-impregnated cloud — cloud above cloud . . . and seems only to increase the beautiful illusion by the infinite variety of decoration in which she revels, binding tree to tree in a tangle of anaconda-like lianas, and dwindling down from these huge cables to airy webs and hairlike fibres that vibrate to the wind of the passing insect's wing.

W. H. Hudson (1841–1922)
Argentine-born English writer

The day has passed delightfully. Delight, however, is a weak term to express the feelings of a naturalist who, for the first time, has wandered by himself in a Brazilian forest. . . . To a person fond of natural history, such a day as this brings with it a deeper pleasure than he can ever hope to experience again.

Charles Darwin (1809–1882)
English naturalist and scientist

THE FOREST

"This must be the wood," [Alice] said thoughtfully to herself, "where things have no names."

Lewis Carroll (Rev. Charles Dodgson, 1832–1898)
English mathematician and writer

This is the forest primeval. The murmuring pines and
   the hemlocks,
Bearded with moss, and in garments green, indistinct in
   the twilight,
Stand like Druids of old.

Henry Wadsworth Longfellow (1807–1882)
American poet

It is a remarkably pleasant occupation, to lie on one's back in a forest and look upwards! It seems that you are looking into a bottomless sea, that it is stretching out far and wide *below* you, that the trees are not rising from the earth but, as if they were the roots of enormous plants, are descending or falling steeply into those lucid, glassy waves . . . .

Ivan Turgenev (1818–1883)
Russian writer

Walking through the woods, you can never see far, either ahead or behind, so you move without much of a sense of getting anywhere or of moving at any certain speed. You burrow through the foliage in the air much as a mole burrows through the roots in the ground.

Wendell Berry (b. 1934)
American poet and writer

The uniformity of a forest soon becomes very wearisome. This west coast makes me remember with pleasure the free, unbounded plains of Patagonia; yet, with the true spirit of

contradiction, I cannot forget how sublime is the silence of the forest.

Charles Darwin (1809–1882)
English naturalist and scientist

Just being in the woods, at night, in the cabin, is something too excellent to be justified or explained! It just is.

Thomas Merton (1915–1968)
American writer and Trappist monk

. . . because the Forest will always be there . . . and anybody who is Friendly with Bears can find it.

A. A. Milne (1882–1956)
English poet and writer

THE SWAMP

Ye marshes, how candid and simple and nothing-with-
     holding and free
Ye publish yourselves to the sky and offer yourselves to
     the sea!

Sidney Lanier (1842–1881)
American poet

145

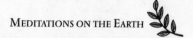

Magic birds were dancing in the mystic marsh. The grass swayed with them, and the shallow waters, and the earth fluttered under them. The earth was dancing with the cranes, and the low sun, and the wind and sky.

Marjorie Kinnan Rawlings (1896–1953)
American writer

Frogs in the marsh mud drone their old lament.

Virgil (70–19 B.C.)
Roman poet

Hope and the future for me are not in lawns and cultivated fields, not in towns and cities, but in the impervious and quaking swamps.

Henry David Thoreau (1817–1862)
American writer

The ground became soft and damp, like volcanic ash, and the vegetation was thicker and thicker, and the cries of the birds and the uproar of the monkeys became more and more remote. . . . They could not return because the strip

146

that they were opening as they went along would soon
close up with a new vegetation that almost seemed to grow
before their eyes.

Gabriel García Márquez (b. 1928)
Colombian writer

THE PRAIRIE

These are the gardens of the Desert, these
The unshorn fields, boundless and beautiful,
For which the speech of England has no name —
The Prairies.

William Cullen Bryant (1794–1878)
American poet

Among the hills and wooded valleys of the East, the
landscape closes in like a bud. Here, on the plains, it
opens out, expands like a flower full-blown.

Edwin Way Teale (1899–1980)
American nature writer

As my eyes
search
the prairie
I feel the summer
in the spring.

Chippewa song

A prairie like that, one big enough to carry the eye clear to
the sinking, rounding horizon, can be as lonely and grand
and simple in its forms as the sea.

Wallace Stegner (1909–1993)
American writer

Mystery whispered in the grass, played in the branches of
trees overhead, was caught up and blown across the
American line in clouds of dust at evening on the prairies.

Sherwood Anderson (1876–1941)
American writer

To one unaccustomed to it, there is something in-
expressibly lonely in the solitude of a prairie.

Washington Irving (1783–1859)
American writer

To make a prairie it takes a clover and one bee,—
One clover, and a bee,
And revery.
The revery alone will do
If bees are few.

Emily Dickinson (1830–1886)
American poet

THE RIVERS AND LAKES

I do not know much about gods; but I think that the river
Is a strong brown god—sullen, untamed and intractable.

T. S. Eliot (1888–1965)
American-born British poet

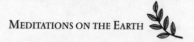

The flow of the river is ceaseless and its water is never
the same.

Kamo No Chomei (1153–1216)
Japanese writer and Buddhist hermit

Rivers perhaps are the only physical features of the world
that are at their best from the air.

Anne Morrow Lindbergh (b. 1907)
American writer

No one has ever seen two rivers that were identical for a
furlong. No one ever will.

Frederic F. Van de Water (1890–1968)
American historian

The sea seems only to pause; the mountain lake to sleep,
and to dream.

John Ruskin (1819–1900)
English critic and essayist

 Landscapes

A lake is the landscape's most beautiful and expressive
feature. It is earth's eye; looking into which the beholder
measures the depth of his own nature.

Henry David Thoreau (1817–1862)
American writer

Floating the rivers takes you through the land, not merely
over its surface . . . this particular form of intimacy . . . can
only be had on the rivers. It flows through your memory
and leaves behind a ripple of emotion: reverence.

Stephen Trimble
20th-century American writer and photographer

To live by a large river is to be kept in the heart of things.

John Haines (b. 1924)
American poet and essayist

Rustle and shimmer of icy creek waters
stones turn underfoot, small and hard on toes . . .
    creek music, heart music,
    smell of sun on gravel.

Gary Snyder (b. 1930)
American poet and nature writer

I've known rivers ancient as the world and older than the
flow of human blood in human veins.

Langston Hughes (1902–1967)
American poet

Never in his life had he seen a river before — this sleek,
sinuous, full-bodied animal, chasing and chuckling,
gripping things with a gurgle and leaving them with a
laugh, to fling itself on fresh playmates that shook
themselves free, and were caught and held again. . . . tired
at last, he sat on the bank, while the river still chattered on
to him, a babbling procession of the best stories in the
world, sent from the heart of the earth to be told at last to
the insatiable sea.

Kenneth Grahame (1859–1932)
English writer

I sat there and forgot and forgot, until what remained was
the river that went by and I who watched. On the river the
heat mirages danced with each other and then they danced

through each other and then they joined hands and danced around each other. Eventually the watcher joined the river, and there was only one of us. I believe it was the river.

Norman Maclean (1902–1990)
American writer

THE SEAS

. . . the sea, once it casts its spell, holds one in its net of wonder forever.

Jacques-Yves Cousteau (b. 1910)
French marine explorer

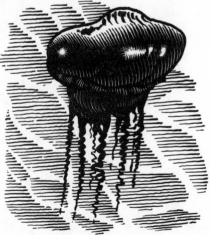

The sea possesses a power over one's moods that has the effect of a will. The sea can hypnotize. Nature in general can do so.

Henrik Ibsen (1828–1906)
Norwegian poet and playwright

153

Of all the things I have ever seen, only the sea is like a
human being; the sky is not, nor the earth. But the sea is
always moving, always something deep in itself is stirring it.
It never rests; it is always wanting, wanting, wanting. It
hurries on; and then it creeps back slowly, without having
reached, moaning. It is always asking a question, and it
never gets the answer.

Olive Schreiner (1855–1920)
South African writer and feminist

The ocean itself seemed full of kingly mountains meeting
or withholding, conflicting, pushing each other aside, part
of a collective immensity that could express itself in the last
little bursting spit of a salt bubble flung out of the foam
that seethed into the beach, a kind of statement of
articulated aim out of a great language still untamed.

John Hay (b. 1915)
American writer

154

 Landscapes

The sea has been called deceitful and treacherous, but
there lies in this trait only the character of a great natural
power, which renews its strength, and, without reference to
joy or sorrow, follows eternal laws which are imposed by a
higher power.

Karl Wilhelm Humboldt (1767–1835)
German philologist and statesman

The sea is feline. It licks your feet—its huge flanks purr very
pleasant for you; but it will crack your bones and eat you,
for all that, and wipe the crimsoned foam from its jaws as if
nothing had happened.

Oliver Wendell Holmes Sr. (1809–1894)
American physician and writer

Love the sea? I dote upon it—from the beach.

Douglas Jerrold (1803–1857)
English humorist and journalist

155

Look out as far as you can see behind the light blue shore
water to where the dark blue water seems to meet the sky.
What you are looking at is not the sea, but only the
sea ceiling.

Mary Lee Settle (b. 1918)
American writer

A sea from which birds travel not within a year, so vast it is
and fearful.

Homer (c. 700 B.C.)
Greek epic poet

And so . . . quietly as the coming dawn, we entered the
solitude of the ocean.

And if we were not annihilated by the contemplation of
such vast adventure it was by grace of that wise providence
of man's nature which, to preserve his reason, lets him be
thoughtless before immensity.

Rockwell Kent (1882–1971)
American artist and writer

156

All I could see was a whole bunch of ocean and wet, messy waves. Though, as it turned out, I was facing the wrong way, and had to clamber and stumble and crawl on all fours over to the Sea Chunder's other railing. There was a whole bunch of ocean on that side, too, if you ask me.

P. J. O'Rourke (b. 1947)
American humorist

I am not exactly pleased with the Atlantic, it is not so majestic as I expected.

Oscar Wilde (1854–1900)
Irish playwright, poet, and writer

I have a seashell collection; maybe you've seen it? I keep it scattered on beaches all over the world.

Steven Wright (b. 1955)
American comedian

157

At sea nothing happens to the sea. Nothing happens to the sky. The sun comes up from the east and goes down to the west. The moon grows from a sickle to an arc lamp, and comes later and later until she is lost in the light as other things are lost in the darkness. After the typhoon, the flying-fish glitter in the sunshine like birds. It's amazing how they get along, all things considered.

George Bernard Shaw (1856–1950)
English playwright and critic

. . . he had not imagined the immense power of the great ocean. The plains of grass seemed to move only when herds of horses, cattle, buffalo stampeded across them; but the plains of water moved always, with a strength greater than any strength he had ever imagined.

Larry McMurtry (b. 1936)
American writer

There is, one knows not what sweet mystery about this sea, whose gently awful stirrings seem to speak of some hidden soul beneath.

Herman Melville (1819–1891)
American writer

158

 Landscapes

I was born by the sea and I have noticed that all the great
events of my life have taken place by the sea. My first idea
of movement, of the dance, certainly came from the
rhythms of the waves.

Isadora Duncan (1878–1927)
American dancer

An everywhere of silver,
With ropes of sand
To keep it from effacing
The track called land.

Emily Dickinson (1830–1886)
American poet

Islands have always fascinated the human mind.
Perhaps it is the instinctive response of man, the land
animal, welcoming a brief intrusion of earth in the vast,
overwhelming expanse of sea.

Rachel Carson (1907–1964)
American biologist and writer

The wind's feet shine along the sea.

Algernon Charles Swinburne (1837–1909)
English poet

There is a perpetual mystery and excitement in living on the seashore, which is in part a return to childhood . . . the child sees the bright shells, the vivid weeds and red sea-anemones of the rock pools with wonder and with the child's eye for minutiae. . . .

Gavin Maxwell (1914–1969)
Scottish nature writer

Let me snuff thee up, sea breeze! and whinny in thy spray.

Herman Melville (1819–1891)
American writer

Who can say of a particular sea that it is old? Distilled by the sun, kneaded by the moon, it is renewed in a year, in a day, or in an hour.

Thomas Hardy (1840–1928)
English novelist and poet

160

 Landscapes

The sea never changes and its works, for all the talk of men, are wrapped in mystery.

Joseph Conrad (1857–1924)
Polish-born English writer

Along the strip of wet sand that marks the ebbing and flowing of the tide, death walks hugely and in many forms. Even the torn fragments of green sponge yield bits of scrambling life striving to return to the great mother that has nourished and protected them.

Loren Eiseley (1907–1977)
American anthropologist and writer

A hundred feet down the fish apparently do not associate us with the surface. In the sad bluish gloom one is accepted in the jungle and its inhabitants have no fear, merely curiosity toward the extraordinary animal with a mania for spreading bubbles.

Jacques-Yves Cousteau (b. 1910)
French marine explorer

If, however, I went to the end of the street, climbed down into a rowboat and started out, the limits of possibility would encircle the whole globe. . . . there is actually open water between my little pier and the edge of the Antarctic barrier, the most distant waves of the Black Sea, the Amazon-drained eatern slopes of the Andes, the arctic foam churned up by swimming polar bears, and the flood of the Red Sea lapping the hot Arabian sands. The garbage-strewn tide swirling around the unlovely piles off my Sixty-seventh Street pier takes on a meaning and a dignity which it never had before.

William Beebe (1877–1962)
American naturalist and explorer

Green Things

People from a planet without flowers would think we must be mad with joy the whole time to have the things about us.

Iris Murdoch (b. 1919)
English novelist and philosopher

We have no reason for denying to the world of plants a certain slow, dim, vague, large, leisurely semi-consciousness.

John Cowper Powys (1872–1963)
English writer

. . . old Indian teaching was that it is wrong to tear loose from its place on the earth anything that may be growing there. It may be cut off, but it should not be uprooted. The trees and grass have spirits.

Wooden Leg
19th-century Native American (Cheyenne) warrior

I am the grass.
Let me work.

Carl Sandburg (1878–1967)
American poet

Grass is the forgiveness of nature — her constant
benediction. Forests decay, harvest perish, flowers vanish,
but grass is immortal.

Brian Ingalls
20th-century American writer

A grass-blade's no easier to make than an oak.

James Russell Lowell (1819–1891)
American poet

It would seem impossible that anyone, however incrusted
with care, could escape the Godful influence of these
sacred fern forests. Yet this very day I saw a shepherd pass
through one of the finest of them without betraying more
feeling than his sheep. "What do you think of these grand
ferns?" I asked. "Oh, they're only d——d big brakes,"
he replied.

John Muir (1838–1914)
Scottish-born American naturalist

 Green Things

What is a weed? A plant whose virtues have not yet
been discovered.

Ralph Waldo Emerson (1803–1882)
American essayist and poet

In a way, nobody sees a flower really, it is so small, we
haven't time — and to see takes time, like to have a friend
takes time.

Georgia O'Keeffe (1887–1986)
American painter

One cannot praise the pond-lily; his best words mar it, like
the insects that eat its petals: but he can contemplate it as it
opens in the morning sun and distills such perfume, such
purity, such snow of petal and such gold of anther, from
the dark water and still darker ooze.

John Burroughs (1837–1921)
American writer and naturalist

Consider the lilies of the field, how they grow; they neither
toil nor spin: yet I tell you, even Solomon in all his glory
was not arrayed like one of these.

Matthew 6:28-29; Luke 12:27.

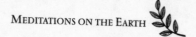

I know a bank whereon the wild thyme blows,
Where oxlips and the nodding violet grows
Quite over-canopied with luscious woodbine,
With sweet musk-roses, and with eglantine:
There sleeps Titania some time of the night,
Lull'd in these flowers with dances and delight.

William Shakespeare (1564–1616)
English playwright and poet

These roses under my window make no reference to
former roses or to better ones; they are for what they are;
they exist with God to-day. There is no time to them.
There is simply the rose; it is perfect in every moment of
its existence.

Ralph Waldo Emerson (1803–1882)
American poet and essayist

 Green Things

Flower in the crannied wall,
I pluck you out of the crannies,
I hold you here, root and all, in my hand,
Little flower — but *if* I could understand
What you are, root and all, and all in all,
I should know what God and man is.

Alfred, Lord Tennyson (1809–1892)
English poet

Wee, modest, crimson-tippèd flow'r,
Thou's met me in an evil hour;
For I maun crush amang the stoure
　　Thy slender stem;
To spare thee now is past my pow'r,
Thou bonie gem.

Robert Burns (1759–1796)
Scottish poet

A little higher, almost at the very head of the pass, I found the blue arctic daisy and purple-flowered bryanthus, the mountain's own darlings, gentle mountaineers face to face with the sky, kept safe and warm by a thousand miracles, seeming always the finer and purer the wilder and stormier their homes.

John Muir (1838–1914)
Scottish-born American naturalist

Can anything compare to the sight of the first yellow violets blooming along a woodland path? These most fragile of plants are yet hardy enough to bloom when nights are still frosty and snow still lingers in the ravines.

Howard Ensign Evans (b. 1919)
American entomologist

A flower's fragrance declares to all the world that it is fertile, available, and desirable, its sex organs oozing with nectar. Its smell reminds us in vestigial ways of fertility, vigor, life-force, all the optimism, expectancy, and

passionate bloom of youth. We inhale its ardent aroma and, no matter what our ages, we feel young and nubile in a world aflame with desire.

Diane Ackerman (b. 1948)
American writer

What a pity flowers can utter no sound!—A singing rose, a whispering violet, a murmuring honeysuckle,—oh, what a rare and exquisite miracle would these be!

Henry Ward Beecher (1813–1887)
American clergyman

To analyze the charms of flowers is like dissecting music; it is one of those things which it is far better to enjoy, than to attempt fully to understand.

Henry Theodore Tuckerman (1813–71)
American critic and writer

169

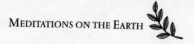

To me the meanest flower that blows can give thoughts
that do often lie too deep for tears.

William Wordsworth (1770–1850)
English poet

Of all man's works of art, a cathedral is greatest. A vast and
majestic tree is greater than that.

Henry Ward Beecher (1813–1887)
American clergyman

Besides the motives that have been mentioned it may be
added that the Great Khan is the more disposed to plant
trees because astrologers tell him that those who plant
trees are rewarded with long life.

Marco Polo (1254–1324)
Italian merchant and traveler

 Green Things

In me the truth of douglas fir, straight, tall,
    strong-trunked land hero of fireproof bark.
Sheltering tree of life, cedar's truth be mine,
    cypress truth, juniper aroma, strength of yew.

Chinook psalter

There was something stubborn about jungle trees,
the way they crowded each other and gave us no shade.
I saw cruelty in the hanging vines and selfishness in their
root systems.

Paul Theroux (b. 1941)
American writer

... the pines seem to me the best interpreters of winds.

John Muir (1838–1914)
Scottish-born nature writer

171

Can you live without a willow tree? Well, no, you can't. The willow tree is you.

John Steinbeck (1902–1968)
American writer

The hurricane months are not so far away, I thought, and saw that tree strike its roots deeper, making ready to fight the wind. Useless. If and when it comes they'll all go. Some of the royal palms stand (she told me). Stripped of their branches, like tall brown pillars, still they stand— defiant. Not for nothing are they called royal.

Jean Rhys (1890–1979)
Dominican-born English writer

172

 Green Things

I like trees because they seem more resigned to the way
they have to live than other things do.

Willa Cather (1876–1947)
American novelist

Those beeches and smooth limes—there was something
enervating in the very sight of them; but the strong
knotted old oaks had no bending languor in them—the
sight of them would give a man some energy.

George Eliot (Mary Anne Evans, 1819–1880)
English novelist

I saw in Louisiana a live-oak growing,
All alone stood it and the moss hung down
    from the branches,
Without any companion it grew there uttering joyous
    leaves of dark green . . . .

Walt Whitman (1819–1892)
American poet

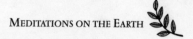

. . . evolution did not intend trees to grow singly. Far more than ourselves they are social creatures, and no more natural as isolated specimens than man is as a marooned sailor or hermit.

John Fowles (b. 1926)
English writer

Except during the nine months before he draws his first breath, no man manages his affairs as well as a tree does.

George Bernard Shaw (1856–1950)
English playwright and writer

For there is hope for a tree,
if it be cut down, that it will sprout again,
and that its shoots will not cease.
Though its root grow old in the earth,

 Green Things

and its stump die in the ground,
yet at the scent of water it will bud
and put forth branches like a young plant.

Job 14:7–9

The wonder is that we can see these trees and not
wonder more.

Ralph Waldo Emerson (1803–1882)
American essayist and poet

Invest in the millenium. Plant sequoias.

Wendell Berry (b. 1934)
American poet and writer

"A Storm in the Forest"

by John Muir (1838–1914)

As a naturalist, explorer, and conservationist, Muir left an enduring legacy. Through his writings and activism, he encouraged the United States to adopt a national conservation policy. One of the fruits of his vision is the Sierra Club, which he founded while lobbying for the establishment of Yosemite National Park.

In this excerpt from The Mountains of California *(1894), Muir reveals some of the wonders he found in the great forests of the West.*

One of the most beautiful and exhilarating storms I ever enjoyed in the Sierra occurred in December, 1874, when I happened to be exploring one of the tributary valleys of the Yuba River. The sky and the ground and the trees had been thoroughly rain-washed and were dry again.

The day was intensely pure, one of those incomparable bits of California winter, warm and balmy and full of white sparkling sunshine, redolent of all the purest influences of the spring, and at the same time enlivened with one of the most bracing wind-storms conceivable. Instead of camping out, as I usually do, I then chanced to be stopping at the house of a friend. But when the storm began to sound, I lost no time in pushing out into the woods to enjoy it. For on such occasions Nature has always something rare to show us, and the danger to life and limb is hardly greater than one would experience crouching deprecatingly beneath a roof.

It was still early morning when I found myself fairly adrift. Delicious sunshine came pouring over the hills, lighting the tops of the pines, and setting free a stream of summery fragrance that contrasted strangely with the wild tones of the storm. The air was mottled with pine-tassels and bright green plumes, that went flashing past in the sunlight like birds pursued. But there was not the slightest dustiness, nothing less pure than leaves, and ripe pollen, and flecks of withered bracken and moss. I heard trees falling for hours at the rate of one every two or three minutes; some uprooted, partly on account of the loose, water-soaked condition of the ground; others broken straight across, where some weakness caused by fire had determined the spot. The gestures of the various trees made a delightful study. . . .

Toward midday, after a long, tingling scramble through copses of hazel and ceanothus, I gained the summit of the highest ridge in the neighborhood; and then it occurred to me that it would be a fine thing to climb one of the trees to obtain a wider outlook and get my ear close to the Aeolian music of its topmost needles. . . . After cautiously casting about, I made choice of the tallest of a group of Douglas Spruces that were growing close together like a tuft of grass, no one of which seemed likely to fall unless all the rest fell with it. Though comparatively young, they were about 100 feet high, and their lithe, brushy tops were rocking and swirling in wild ecstasy. Being accustomed to climb trees in making botanical studies, I experienced no difficulty in reaching the top of this one, and never before did I enjoy so noble an exhilaration of motion. The slender tops

fairly flapped and swished in the passionate torrent, bending and swirling backward and forward, round and round, tracing indescribable combinations of vertical and horizontal curves, while I clung with muscles firm braced, like a bobolink on a reed.

In its widest sweeps my tree-top described an arc of from twenty to thirty degrees, but I felt sure of its elastic temper, having seen others of the same species still more severely tried—bent almost to the ground indeed, in heavy snows—without breaking a fiber. I was therefore safe, and free to take the wind into my pulses and enjoy the excited forest from my superb outlook. The view from here must be extremely beautiful in any weather. Now my eye roved over the piny hills and dales as over fields of waving grain, and felt the light running in ripples and broad swelling undulations across the valleys from ridge to ridge, as the shining foliage was stirred by corresponding waves of air. Oftentimes these waves of reflected light would break up suddenly into a kind of beaten foam, and again, after chasing one another in regular order, they would seem to bend forward in concentric curves, and disappear on some hillside, like sea-waves on a shelving shore. The quantity of light reflected from the bent needles was so great as to make whole groves appear as if covered with snow, while the black shadows beneath the trees greatly enhanced the effect of the silvery splendor. . . .

The wounds of the storm corresponded gloriously with this wild exuberance of light and motion. The profound bass of the naked branches and boles booming like waterfalls; the quick, tense vibrations of the pine-needles, now rising to a shrill, whistling hiss, now falling to a silky murmur; the rustling of laurel groves in the dells, and the keen metallic click of leaf on leaf—all this was heard in easy analysis when the attention was calmly bent. . . .

I kept my lofty perch for hours, frequently closing my eyes to enjoy the music by itself, or to feast quietly on the delicious fragrance that was streaming past. The fragrance of the woods was less marked than that produced during warm rain, when so many balsamic buds and leaves are steeped like tea; but, from the chafing of resiny branches against each other, and the incessant attrition of myriads of needles, the gale was spiced to a very tonic degree. And besides the fragrance from these local sources there were traces of scents brought from afar. For this wind came first from the sea, rubbing against its fresh, briny waves, then distilled through the redwoods, threading rich ferny gulches, and spreading itself in broad undulating currents over many a flower-enameled ridge of the coast mountains, then across the golden plains, up the purple foot-hills, and into these piny woods with the varied incense gathered by the way. . . .

We all travel the milky way together, trees and men; but it never occurred to me until this stormday, while swinging in the wind, that trees are travelers, in the ordinary sense. They make many journeys, not extensive ones, it is true; but our own little journeys, away and back again, are only little more than tree-wavings—many of them not so much.

When the storm began to abate, I dismounted and sauntered down through the calming woods. The storm-tones died away, and, turning toward the east, I beheld the countless hosts of the forest hushed and tranquil, towering above one another on the slopes of the hills like a devout audience. The setting sun filled them with amber light, and seemed to say, while they listened, "My peace I give unto you."

The Animal Kingdom

All that is comprehended of flesh and of spirit of life and so of body and soul is called animal — a beast — whether it be airy as fowls that fly, or watery as fish that swim, or earthy as beasts that go on the ground and in fields, as men and beasts, wild and tame, or other that creep and glide on the ground.

Bartholomew the Englishman
13th-century English friar

In a world older and more complete than ours they move finished and complete, gifted with extensions of the senses we have lost or never attained, living by voices we shall never hear. They are not brethren, they are not underlings; they are other nations, caught with ourselves in the net of life and time, fellow prisoners of the splendour and travail of the earth.

Henry Beston (1888–1968)
American nature writer

 The Animal Kingdom

All of us, I think, were conscious of that warm sense
of privilege you get when you are lucky enough to watch,
close up, as truly wild animals go about their quiet
business.

Colin Fletcher (b. 1922)
Welsh hiker and writer

I think I could turn and live with animals, they're so placid
   and self-contained,
I stand and look at them long and long. . . .

Walt Whitman (1819–1892)
American poet

. . . something eerie ties us to the world of animals.
Sometimes the animals pull you backward into it. You
share hunger and fear with them like salt in blood.

Barry Lopez (b. 1945)
American writer

183

Animals have a prodigious advantage over us: they foresee neither evils nor death.

Voltaire (1694–1778)
French writer and philosopher

The best thing about animals is that they don't talk much.

Thornton Wilder (1897–1975)
American writer

FROM THE SMALLEST TO THE LARGEST

Nature is to be found in her entirety nowhere more than in her smallest creatures.

Pliny the Elder (A.D. 23–79)
Roman scholar

Four things on earth are small,
but they are exceedingly wise:
the ants are a people not strong,
yet they provide their food in the summer;

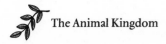

the badgers are a people not mighty,
yet they make their homes in the rocks;
the locusts have no king,
yet all of them march in rank,
the lizard you can take in your hands,
yet it is in kings' palaces.

Proverbs 30:24–28

There is as much to be discovered and to astonish in
magnifying an insect as a star.

Thaddeus William Harris (1795–1856)
American entomologist

The most insignificant insects and reptiles are of much
more consequence, and have much more influence in the
economy of nature, than the incurious are aware of; and
are mighty in their effect, from their minuteness, which
renders them less an object of attention; and from their
numbers and fecundity.

Gilbert White (1720–1793)
English clergyman

... most elegantly finished in all parts, [the hummingbird]
is a miniature work of our Great Parent, who seems to have
formed it the smallest, and at the same time the most
beautiful of the winged species.

Hector St. John de Crèvecoeur (1735–1813)
French-born American farmer and writer

If I spent enough time with the tiniest creature —
even a caterpillar —
I would never have to prepare a sermon.

Meister Eckhart (1260–1327)
German theologian

A very little thing, a little worm,
Or hourglass-blazoned spider, it is said,
　　Can kill a tiger.

Robert Lowell (1917–1977)
American poet

 The Animal Kingdom

Is it not curious that so vast a being as the whale should see the world through so small an eye, and hear the thunder through an ear which is smaller than a hare's?

Herman Melville (1819–1891)
American writer

Even at rest the [elephant] herd flowed in perpetual motion, the ears like delicate great petals, the ripple of the mud-caked flanks, the coiling trunks — a dream rhythm, a rhythm of wind and trees.

Peter Matthiessen (b. 1927)
American writer

There Leviathan
Hugest of living creatures, on the deep
Stretch'd like a promontory sleeps or swims,
And seems a moving land, and at his gills
Draws in, and at his trunk spouts out a sea.

John Milton (1608–1674)
English poet

Human beings possess such immense powers that few animals cause us to feel truly humble. A whale does, swimming beside you, as big as a reclining building, its eye carefully observing you. It could easily devastate you with a twitch, and yet it doesn't.

Diane Ackerman (b. 1948)
American writer

ON MANY LEGS

[Insects] are not only cold-blooded, and green- and yellow-blooded, but are also cased in a clacking horn. . . . They have rigid eyes and brains strung down their backs. But they make up the bulk of our comrades-at-life, so I look to them for a glimmer of companionship.

Annie Dillard (b. 1945)
American writer

And that was another gap between us. Between all men and all insects. We humans, saddled for a lifetime with virtually the same body, naturally find it difficult to imagine a life in

which you can, at a single stroke, outside a fairy tale,
just by splitting your skin and stepping out, change into
something utterly different.

Colin Fletcher (b. 1922)
Welsh hiker and writer

The butterfly lures us not only because he is beautiful, but
because he is transitory. The caterpillar is uglier, but in him
we can regard the better joy of becoming.

Cynthia Ozick (b. 1928)
American writer

Then there is that other appeal, the stronger one, of
spending, during certain parts of the year, a ten- or twelve-
hour working day with bees, which are, when all is said and
done, simply a bunch of bugs. But spending my days in
close and intimate contact with creatures who are
structured so differently from humans, and who get
on with life in such a different way, is like being a visitor
in an alien but ineffably engaging world.

Sue Hubbell (b. 1935)
American beekeeper and writer

To-day I saw the dragon-fly
Come from the wells where he did lie.

An inner impulse rent the veil
Of his old husk; from head to tail
Came out clear plates of sapphire mail.

He dried his wings; like gauze they grew;
Thro' crofts and pastures wet with dew
A living flash of light he flew.

Alfred, Lord Tennyson (1809–1892)
English poet

 The Animal Kingdom

And what's a butterfly? At best,
He's but a caterpillar, drest.

John Gay (1685–1732)
English poet and playwright

Who when examining in the cabinet of the entomologist
the gay exotic butterflies, and singular cicadas, will associate with these lifeless objects, the ceaseless harsh music of
the latter, and the lazy flight of the former, — the sure ac-
companiments of the still, glowing noonday of the tropics?

Charles Darwin (1809–1882)
English naturalist and scientist

Only the grasshoppers made a combined whirring, as if
infuriated — such an oppressive, unceasing, insipid, dry
sound. It was appropriate to the unabating, midday heat, as
if literally engendered by it, literally summoned by it out of
the sun-smelted earth.

Ivan Turgenev (1818–1883)
Russian writer

The honey-bee's great ambition is to be rich, to lay up great stores, to possess the sweet of every flower that blooms. She is more than provident. Enough will not satisfy her; she must have all she can get by hook or by crook.

John Burroughs (1837–1921)
American writer and naturalist

The mosquito knows full well, small as he is he's a beast of prey.

D. H. Lawrence (1885–1930)
English poet and novelist

My attraction for mosquitoes is so great that people who have some reason to walk near stagnant ponds or swampy marshes sometimes ask me along as a means of drawing off attackers . . . .

Calvin Trillin (b. 1935)
American writer

Then in a wailful choir the small gnats mourn
   Among the river shallows, borne aloft
      Or sinking as the light wind lives or dies.

John Keats (1795–1821)
English poet

The Mantis has in store for us, in her relations with her
own kith and kin, manners even more atrocious than those
prevailing among the Spiders, who have an evil reputation
in this respect.

Jean Henri Fabre (1823–1915)
French entomologist

Not one of us could have planned the fly, not one of us
could have constructed him; and no one would have
considered it wise to try, except under an assumed name.

Mark Twain (Samuel Clemens, 1835–1910)
American novelist

193

Go to the ant, O sluggard;
consider her ways, and be wise.
Without having any chief,
officer or ruler,
she prepares her food in summer,
and gathers her sustenance in harvest.

Proverbs 6:6–8

One thing I'd like to know most of all: when those ants
have made the Hill, and are all there, touching and
exchanging, and the whole mass begins to behave like
a single huge creature, and *thinks*, what on earth is that
thought? And while you're at it, I'd like to know a second
thing: when it happens, does any single ant know about it?
Does his hair stand on end?

Lewis Thomas (b. 1913)
American biologist and writer

Moths that fly by day are not properly to be called moths;
they do not excite that pleasant sense of dark autumn

194

 The Animal Kingdom

nights and ivy-blossom which the commonest yellow-
underwing asleep in the shadow of the curtain never fails
to arouse in us.

Virginia Woolf (1882–1941)
English novelist

Everything belonging to the spider is admirable.

Jonathan Edwards (1703–1758)
American theologian

Earth-worms, though in appearance a small and despicable
link in the chain of nature, yet, if lost, would make a
lamentable chasm. . . . the earth without worms would
soon become cold, hard-bound, and void of fermentation;
and consequently sterile . . . .

Gilbert White (1720–1793)
English clergyman

195

THE FISH

O for the swiftness and balance of fishes!

Walt Whitman (1819–1892)
American poet

I could never be talked into believing that all a fish knows is hunger and fear. In fact, I go so far sometimes as to imagine that a fish thinks pretty thoughts. Before I made the cast, I imagined the fish with the black back lying cool in the carbonated water full of bubbles from the waterfalls. He was looking downriver and watching the foam with food in it backing upstream like a floating cafeteria coming to wait on its customers. And he probably was imagining that the speckled foam was eggnog with nutmeg sprinkled on it.

Norman Maclean (1902–1990)
American writer

From the data, covering over a hundred shark encounters with many varieties, I can offer two conclusions: The better

196

acquainted we become with sharks, the less we know them, and one can never tell what a shark is going to do.

Jacques-Yves Cousteau (b. 1910)
French marine explorer

Some divers talk so much about sharks that you would think they were the only fish in the sea. It is as if the beautiful great land forests were described only in terms of poisonous snakes and panthers. Can you imagine going into the woods aware only of those animals, so that you miss the calmness and the thousands of other animals, the beautiful and the shy?

Mary Lee Settle (b. 1918)
American writer

For thousands upon thousands of years the salmon have known and followed these threads of fresh water that leads [from the ocean] back to the rivers, each returning to the tributary in which it spent the first months or years of life.

Rachel Carson (1907–1964)
American biologist and writer

THE REPTILES

A narrow fellow in the grass
Occasionally rides;
You may have met him, — did you not,
His notice sudden is.

The grass divides as with a comb,
A spotted shaft is seen;
And then it closes at your feet
And opens further on.

Emily Dickinson (1830–1886)
American poet

Ask a toad what is beauty—the great beauty, the *to kalon*; he will answer that it is the female with two great round eyes coming out of her little head, her large flat mouth, her yellow belly, and brown back . . . .

Voltaire (1694–1778)
French writer and philosopher

Alligators are creatures of the water's edge who have dual citizenship in the wet and dry worlds. Though not technically amphibians, they live in a similiar twilight of water and sky, and they are masters of the narrow realm where the two worlds collide.

Diane Ackerman (b. 1948)
American writer

In the decline of the year, [the turtle] improves the faint autumnal beams by getting within the reflection of a fruit wall; and, though he never has read that planes inclined to the horizon receive a greater share of warmth, he inclines his shell, by tilting it against the wall, to collect and admit every feeble ray.

Gilbert White (1720–1793)
English clergyman

No two turtles ever lunched together with the idea of promoting anything. . . . Turtles do not work day and night to perfect explosive devices that wipe out Pacific islands and eventually render turtles sterile. Turtles never use the word "implementation" or the phrases "hard core" and "in the last analysis." No turtle ever rang another turtle back on the phone. In the last analysis, a turtle, although lacking know-how, knows how to live.

E. B. White (1899–1985)
American essayist

THE BIRDS

How do you know but that every bird that cleaves the aerial way is not an immense world of delight closed to your senses five?

William Blake (1757–1827)
English poet and artist

It is not only fine feathers that make fine birds.

Aesop (c. 550 B.C.)
Greek fabulist

 The Animal Kingdom

A bird does not sing because it has an answer—it sings
because it has a song.

Ancient Chinese proverb

He himself loved all natural sounds in the bush and the
desert, but he had to admit none equalled the sounds of
birds. It was as if the sky made music in their throats and
one could hear the sun rise and set, the night fall and the
first stars come out in their voices.

Laurens Van Der Post (b. 1906)
South African writer

In order to see birds it is necessary to become a part of
the silence.

Robert Lynd (1879–1949)
Irish journalist

The language of birds is very ancient, and, like other ancient modes of speech, very elliptical: little is said, but much is meant and understood.

Gilbert White (1720–1793)
English clergyman

Many people won't know what to say when the ducks show up, but I will. Maybe I'll say, "Oh ducks, oh ducks, oh ducks," or just "Ducks wonderful ducks!" I practice these sayings every day, and even though the ducks haven't come yet, when they do, I'll know what to say.

Steve Martin (b. 1945)
American actor and comedian

Once birds sang and flirted among the leaves while men, more helpless and less accomplished, skulked between the trunks below them. Now they linger in the few trees that

men have left standing, or fit themselves into the chinks
of the human world, into its church towers, lamp-posts,
and gutters.

Jacquetta Hawkes (b. 1910)
English archaeologist and writer

The wrinkled sea beneath [the eagle] crawls;
He watches from his mountain walls,
And like a thunderbolt he falls.

Alfred, Lord Tennyson (1809–1892)
English poet

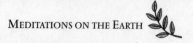

... your Londoners are very fond of talking about the bird
& I believe fancy every bird they hear after sunset a
Nightingale ...

John Clare (1793–1864)
English poet

I rejoice that there are owls. Let them do the idiotic and
maniacal hooting for men.

Henry David Thoreau (1817–1862)
American writer

The swallow of summer, she toils all summer,
A blue-dark knot of glittering voltage,
A whiplash swimmer, a fish of the air.

Ted Hughes (b. 1930)
British poet

204

The duck spreads oil on its feathers with its beak from a small sac above the tail. The feathers then lie smooth and waterproof, reminding us that we too must take time to care for our bodies and equipment.

Marianne Moore (1887–1972)
American poet

Geese, we have found, are alert and articulate and they practically never sleep, but they are also undiscriminating, gossipy, and as easily diverted as children.

E. B. White (1899–1985)
American essayist

To write honestly and with conviction anything about the migration of birds, one should oneself have migrated. Somehow or other we should dehumanize ourselves, feel the feel of feathers on our body and wind in our wings, and finally know what it is to leave abundance and safety and daylight and yield to a compelling instinct, age-old, seeming at the time quite devoid of reason and object.

William Beebe (1877–1962)
American naturalist and explorer

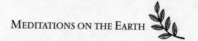

I once had a sparrow alight upon my shoulder for a
moment while I was hoeing in a village garden, and I felt
that I was more distinguished by that circumstance than I
should have been by any epaulet I could have worn.

Henry David Thoreau (1817–1862)
American writer

THE MAMMALS

Deer, otter, foxes are messengers from another condition
of life, another mentality, and bring us tidings of places
where we don't go.

Edward Hoagland (b. 1932)
American writer

206

 The Animal Kingdom

Hundreds of zebras walk the skyline. They become
animated heat waves.

Terry Tempest Williams (b. 1955)
American nature writer

I had time after time watched the progression across
the plain of the Giraffe, in their queer, inimitable,
vegetative gracefulness, as if it were not a herd of animals
but a family of rare, long-stemmed, speckled gigantic
flowers slowly advancing.

Isak Dinesen (Karen Blixen, 1883–1962)
Danish-born writer

If you should ever have to do any waiting where there are
sloths, I can recommend watching them as a way to pass
the time. It is as good as reading *War and Peace*—it never
gives out on you.

Archie Carr (1909–1987)
American biologist and writer

. . . for all the motions of a squirrel, even in the most solitary recesses of the forest, imply spectators as much as those of a dancing girl . . . before you could say Jack Robinson, he would be in the top of a young pitch pine, winding up his clock and chiding all imaginary spectators, soliloquizing and talking to all the universe at the same time,—for no reason that I could ever detect, or he himself was aware of, I suspect.

Henry David Thoreau (1817–1862)
American writer

And a mouse is miracle enough to stagger sextillions of infidels.

Walt Whitman (1819–1892)
American poet

All knowledge, the totality of all questions and all answers, is contained in the dog.

Franz Kafka (1883–1924)
Czechoslovakian writer

208

 The Animal Kingdom

Delicate mother Kangaroo
Sitting up there rabbit-wise, but huge, plumb-weighted,
And lifting her beautiful slender face, oh! so much more
    gently and finely lined than a rabbit's, or a hare's . . . .

D. H. Lawrence (1885–1930)
English poet and novelist

The elephant is the wisest of all animals, the only one who
remembers his former lives; and he remains motionless for
long periods of time, meditating thereon.

Ancient Buddhist text

Look at a tiger. The light and dark of his stripes and the
black edge encircling the white patch on his ear help him
to look like the jungle with flecks of sun on it.

Marianne Moore (1887–1972)
American poet

209

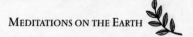

Quick as a breath, quiet as a whisper, the doe glides off into
the forest. Sometimes when I see a deer this way I know it
is real at the moment, but afterward it seems like a dream.

Richard K. Nelson (b. 1941)
American anthropologist

To tell the truth, we have never met animals who have
made the transition from land to water (sea lions, sperm
whales, dolphins, etc.) without feeling a touch of envy.

Jacques-Yves Cousteau (b. 1910)
French marine explorer

Heavens Above

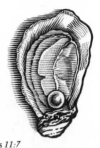

Light is sweet, and it is pleasant for the eyes to behold
the sun.

Ecclesiastes 11:7

How the sun silently mounts in the broad clear sky, on his
day's journey! How the warm beams bathe all, and come
streaming kissingly and almost hot on my face.

Walt Whitman (1819–1892)
American poet

Little soft clouds played happily in a blue sky, skipping
from time to time in front of the sun as if they had come to
put it out, and then sliding away suddenly so that the next
might have his turn.

A. A. Milne (1882–1956)
English poet and writer

But contemplate the sky, it's there to be contemplated. A
mild shock to see it so blank, blue, a thin airy ghostly blue,
no clouds to disguise its emptiness.

Joyce Carol Oates (b. 1938)
American writer

Why make so much of fragmentary blue
In here and there a bird, or butterfly,
Or flower, or wearing-stone, or open eye,
When heaven presents in sheets the solid hue?

Robert Frost (1874–1963)
American poet

Taken all in all, the sky is a miraculous achievement. It
works, and for what it is designed to accomplish it is as
infallible as anything in nature.

Lewis Thomas (b. 1913)
American physician and writer

212

 Heavens Above

I [a cloud] am the daughter of Earth and Water,
And the nursling of the Sky;
I pass through the pores of the ocean and shores,
I change, but I cannot die.

Percy Bysshe Shelley (1792–1822)
English poet

The clouds are children of the heavens, and when they play
among the rocks they lift them to the region above.

John Wesley Powell (1834–1902)
American explorer

How air is azurèd;
O how! nay do but stand
Where you can lift your hand
Skywards: rich, rich it laps
Round the four fingergaps.

Gerard Manley Hopkins (1844–1889)
English poet and Jesuit priest

213

Haven't you sometimes seen a cloud that looked like
   a centaur?
Or a leopard perhaps? Or a wolf? Or a bull?

Aristophanes (c. 450–385 B.C.)
Greek playwright

We lift our eyes from the city horizon and let them play
over the entire hemisphere of the sky—the home of day
and night, of auroras, clouds, storms, sun, planets and
stars. And now we begin to feel less the lords of creation.
A gull soars easily past, bound for the utmost rim of our
circle, and we begin humbly to take stock of our puny feats
within celestial space.

William Beebe (1877–1962)
American naturalist and explorer

Be praised my lord with all your creatures
but especially with Brother Sun
because you show us light and day through him

and he is lovely glowing with great shine
from you my lord: his definition.

St. Francis of Assisi (1182–1226)
Founder of Franciscan order

The glorious sun,—the centre and soul of our system,—the
lamp that lights it—the fire that heats it,—the magnet that
guides and controls it;—the fountain of color, which gives
its azure to the sky, its verdure to the fields, its rainbow-
hues to the gay world of flowers, and the purple light of
love to the marble cheek of youth and beauty.

Sir David Brewster (1781–1868)
Scottish physicist

The sun too penetrates into privies, but is not polluted
by them.

Diogenes (c. 400–c. 325 B.C.)
Greek philosopher

215

... the setting sun as a traveller glad to rest was leaning his
enlarged rim on the earth like a table of fire ...

John Clare (1793–1864)
English poet

The sun is at home on the plains. Precisely there does it
have the certain character of a god.

N. Scott Momaday (b. 1934)
American writer

We had the sky, up there, all speckled with stars, and we
used to lay on our backs and look up at them, and discuss
about whether they was made, or only just happened—Jim
he allowed they was made, but I allowed they just

happened; I judged it would have took too long to *make* so
many. Jim said the moon could a *laid* them; well, that
looked kind of reasonable. . . .

Mark Twain (Samuel Clemens, 1835–1910)
American humorist and writer

Don't carry a lantern in moonlight.

Japanese proverb

The moon like a flower
In heaven's high bower,
With silent delight
Sits and smiles on the night.

William Blake (1757–1827)
English poet and artist

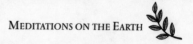

The man who has seen the rising moon break out of the clouds at midnight, has been present like an archangel at the creation of light and of the world.

Ralph Waldo Emerson (1803–1882)
American poet and essayist

Clouds come from time to time—
and bring a chance to rest
from looking at the moon.

Basho (1664–1694)
Japanese Haiku poet

In every country the moon keeps ever the rule of alliance with the sea which it once for all has agreed upon.

The Venerable Bede (673–735)
English scholar and theologian

 Heavens Above

Silently one by one, in the
  infinite meadows of
  heaven
Blossomed the lovely stars,
  the forget-me-nots of the
  angels.

Henry Wadsworth Longfellow (1807–1882)
American poet

The kingly brilliance of Sirius pierced the eye with a steely
glitter, the star called Capella was yellow, Aldebaran and
Betelgeux shone with a fiery red. To persons standing
alone on a hill during a clear midnight such as this, the roll
of the world eastward is almost a palpable movement.

Thomas Hardy (1840–1928)
English novelist and poet

219

It is only possible to conceive how immense and limitless is the sky, either at sea or in the steppe at night when the moon is shining. It is fearful, beautiful, inviting, looks languid, beckons to one till one turns giddy with its blandishments.

Anton Chekhov (1860–1904)
Russian playwright and story writer

The bright suns I see and the dark suns I cannot see are in their place.

Walt Whitman (1819–1892)
American poet

The contemplation of night should lead to elevating rather than to depressing ideas. Who can fix his mind on transitory and earthly things, in presence of those

220

glittering myriads of worlds; and who can dread death or solitude in the midst of this brilliant, animated universe, composed of countless suns and worlds, all full of life and motion?

Jean Paul Richter (1763–1826)
German humorist

A meteor bursts over my head. It's not a shower but a strike, a high fly ball hit hard. . . . though secretly I thought of the "falling stars" as eyes searching the sea, attracted by our boat's running lights.

Gretel Ehrlich (b. 1946)
American writer and rancher

A star is beautiful; it affords pleasure, not from what it is to do, or to give, but simply by being what it is. It befits the heavens; it has congruity with the mighty space in which it dwells. It has repose; no force disturbs its eternal peace. It has freedom; no obstruction lies between it and infinity.

Thomas Carlyle (1795–1881)
Scottish historian and essayist

221

Poor thin crescent
Shivering and twisted high
In the bitter dark.

Issa (1763–1827)
Japanese poet

When we are chafed and fretted by small cares, a look at
the stars will show us the littleness of our own interests.

Maria Mitchell (1818–1889)
American astronomer

The stars hang bright above, silent, as if they watched the
sleeping earth.

Samuel Taylor Coleridge (1772–1834)
English poet

222

 Heavens Above

One sun by day; by night ten thousand shine,
And light us deep into the deity.—
How boundless in magnificence and might!—

Edward Young (1683–1765)
English poet

To a boy, it is something new and beautiful to piss among
the stars. Not under the stars but among them. Even at
night great winds seem always to blow on great mountains,
and tops of trees bend, but, as the boy stands there with
nothing to do but watch, seemingly the sky itself bends and
the stars blow down through the trees until the Milky Way
becomes lost in some distant forest.

Norman Maclean (1902–1990)
American writer

Stars scribble in our eyes the frosty sagas,
The gleaming cantos of unvanquished space.

Hart Crane (1899–1932)
American poet

Put three grains of sand inside a vast cathedral, and the cathedral will be more closely packed with sand than space is with stars.

Sir James Jeans, F.R.S. (1877–1946)
British astronomer and writer

. . . fire is the silent language of the star.

Conrad Aiken (1899–1973)
American poet and critic

Stars are like animals in the wild. We may see the young but never the actual birth, which is a veiled and secret event.

Heinz R. Pagels (1939–1988)
American physicist and writer

 Heavens Above

What if one moon has come and gone with its world of poetry, its weird teachings, its oracular suggestions,—so divine a creature freighted with hints for me, and I have not used her? One moon gone by unnoticed?

Henry David Thoreau (1817–1862)
American writer

On a clear moonless night in midwinter or midsummer, a plume of starlight rises motionless behind the scattering of constellations. . . . The Milky Way is our island universe. . . .

Charles A. Whitney (b. 1929)
American astronomer and writer

If the stars should appear one night in a thousand years, how would men believe and adore; and preserve for generations the remembrance of the city of God which had been shown! But every night come out these envoys of beauty, and light the universe with their admonishing smile.

Ralph Waldo Emerson (1803–1882)
American poet and essayist

"Total Eclipse"

by Annie Dillard, b. 1945

A writer experienced in many genres, Dillard burst upon the scene with the publication of Pilgrim at Tinker Creek, *an exploration of the natural world that won the Pulitzer Prize in 1974. Dillard's willingness to consider nature in all its guises has always distinguished her writing. This excerpt from* Teaching a Stone to Talk *(1982) relates the strange internal and external events that can accompany a solar eclipse.*

It began with no ado. It was odd that such a well-advertised public event should have no starting gun, no overture, no introductory speaker. I should have known right then that I was out of my depth. Without pause or preamble, silent as orbits, a piece of the sun went away. We

looked at it through welders' goggles. A piece of the sun was missing; in its place we saw empty sky.

I had seen a partial eclipse in 1970. A partial eclipse is very interesting. It bears almost no relation to a total eclipse. Seeing a partial eclipse bears the same relation to seeing a total eclipse as kissing a man does to marrying him, or as flying in an airplane does to falling out of an airplane. Although the one experience precedes the other, it in no way prepares you for it. During a partial eclipse the sky does not darken—not even with 94 percent of the sun is hidden. Nor does the sun, seen colorless through protective devices, seem terribly strange. We have all seen a sliver of light in the sky; we have all seen the crescent moon by day. However, during a partial eclipse the air does indeed get cold, precisely as if someone were standing between you and the fire. And blackbirds do fly back to their roosts. I had seen a partial eclipse before, and here was another.

What you see in an eclipse is entirely different from what you know. It is especially different for those of us whose grasp of astronomy is so frail that, given a flashlight, a grapefruit, two oranges, and fifteen years, we still could not figure out which way to set the clocks for Daylight Saving Time. Usually it is a bit of a trick to keep your knowledge from blinding you. But during an eclipse it is easy. What you see is much more convincing than any wild-eyed theory you may know.

You may read that the moon has something to do with eclipses. I have never seen the moon yet. You do not see the moon. So near the sun, it is as completely invisible as the stars are by day. What you see before your eyes is the sun going through phases. It gets narrower and narrower, as the waning moon does, and, like the ordinary moon, it travels alone in the simple sky. The sky is of course background. It does not appear to eat the sun; it is far behind the sun. The sun simply shaves away; gradually, you see less sun and more sky.

The sky's blue was deepening, but there was no darkness. The sun was a wide crescent, like a segment of tangerine. The wind freshened and blew steadily over the hill. The eastern hill across the highway grew dusky and sharp. The towns and orchards in the valley to the south were

dissolving into the blue light. Only the thin river held a trickle of sun.

Now the sky to the west deepened to indigo, a color never seen. A dark sky usually loses color. This was a saturated, deep indigo, up in the air. Stuck up into that unworldly sky was the cone of Mount Adams, and the alpenglow was upon it. The alpenglow is that red light of sunset which holds out on snowy mountaintops long after the valleys and tablelands are dimmed. "Look at Mount Adams," I said, and that was the last sane moment I remember.

I turned back to the sun. It was going. The sun was going, and the world was wrong. The grasses were wrong; they were platinum. Their every detail of stem, head, and blade shone lightless and artificially distinct as an art photographer's platinum print. This color has never been seen on earth. The hues were metallic; their finish was matte. The hillside was a nineteenth-century tinted photograph from which the tints had faded. All the people you see in the photograph, distinct and detailed as their faces look, are now dead. The sky was navy blue. My hands were silver. All the distant hills' grasses were finespun metal which the wind laid down. I was watching a faded color print of a movie filmed in the Middle Ages; I was standing in it, by some mistake. I was standing in a movie of hillside grasses filmed in the Middle Ages. I missed my own century, the people I knew, and the real light of day. . . .

From all the hills came screams. A piece of sky beside the crescent sun was detaching. It was a loosened circle of evening sky, suddenly lighted from the back. It was an abrupt black body out of nowhere; it was a flat disk; it was almost over the sun. That is when there were screams. At once this disk of sky slid over the sun like a lid. The sky snapped over the sun like a lens cover. The hatch in the brain slammed. Abruptly it was dark night, on the land and in the sky. In the night sky was a tiny ring of light. The hole where the sun belongs is very small. A thin ring of light marked its place. There was no sound. The eyes dried, the arteries drained, the lungs hushed. There was no world. We were the world's dead people rotating and orbiting around

and around, embedded in the planet's crust, while the earth rolled down. Our minds were light-years distant, forgetful of almost everything. Only an extraordinary act of will could recall to us our former, living selves and our contexts in matter and time. We had, it seems, loved the planet and loved our lives, but could no longer remember the way of them. We got the light wrong. In the sky was something that should not be there. In the black sky was a ring of light. It was a thin ring, an old, thin silver wedding band, an old, worn ring. It was an old wedding band in the sky, or a morsel of bone. There were stars. It was all over.

The View from Space

Out there in the Milky Way and the world without end Amen, America was a tiny speck of a country, a nickel tossed into the Grand Canyon, and American culture the amount of the Pacific Ocean you bring home in your swimsuit.

Garrison Keillor (b. 1942)
American humorist

How strange and wonderful is our home, our earth, with its swirling vaporous atmosphere, its flowing and frozen liquids, its trembling plants, its creeping, crawling, climbing creatures, the croaking things with wings that hang on rocks and soar through fog, the furry grass, the scaly seas.

Edward Abbey (1927–1989)
American writer

Mountain ranges, volcanoes appeared in salt-and-flour relief. . . . I became an instant believer in plate tectonics. . . .

 The View from Space

The view from overhead makes theory come alive.

Sally Ride (b. 1951)
American astronaut

See revolving the globe,
The ancestor-continents away group'd together,
The present and future continents north and south, with
    the isthmus between.

Walt Whitman (1819–1892)
American poet

But if a man would be alone, let him look at the stars. The rays that come from those heavenly worlds will separate between him and what he touches. One might think the atmosphere was made transparent with this design, to give man, in the heavenly bodies, the perpetual presence of the sublime.

Ralph Waldo Emerson (1803–1882)
American poet and essayist

For Pico [della Mirandola, a Renaissance writer], the world is a limited place, bounded by actual crystal walls, and a material firmament; it is like a painted toy. . . . How different from this childish dream is our own conception of nature, with its unlimited space, its innumerable suns, and the earth but a mote in the beam; how different the strange new awe and superstition with which it fills our minds!

Walter Pater (1839–1894)
English critic

We find that we live on an insignificant planet of a humdrum star, lost in a galaxy tucked away in some forgotten corner of a universe in which there are far more galaxies than people.

Carl Sagan (b. 1934)
American astronomer and writer

The distances between the stars are huge compared with the sizes of the stars: a golf ball in Boston, two golf balls and a pea in Cincinnati, a marble in Miami, a basketball in San Francisco.

Chet Raymo (b. 1936)
American astronomer and writer

 The View from Space

The silence of those infinite spaces terrifies me.

Blaise Pascal (1623–1662)
French scientist and philosopher

This world itself, travelling blindly and swiftly in
overcrowded space, among a million other worlds
travelling blindly and swiftly in contrary directions, may
very well come by a knock that would set it into explosion
like a penny squib.

Robert Louis Stevenson (1850–1894)
Scottish novelist and poet

When I gaze into the stars, they look down upon me
with pity from their serene and silent spaces, like eyes
glistening with tears over the little lot of man. Thousands
of generations, all as noisy as our own, have been swal-
lowed up by time, and there remains no record of them
any more. Yet Arcturus and Orion, Sirius and Pleiades, are
still shining in their courses, clear and young, as when the
shepherd first noted them in the plain of Shinar!

Thomas Carlyle (1795–1881)
Scottish historian and essayist

Human Nature

I'm truly sorry man's dominion
Has broken Nature's social union.

Robert Burns (1759–1796)
Scottish poet

To gild refined gold, to paint the lily,
To throw a perfume on the violet,
To smooth the ice, or add another hue
Unto the rainbow, or with taper-light
To seek the beauteous eye of heaven to garnish,
Is wasteful and ridiculous excess.

William Shakespeare (1564–1616)
English playwright and poet

... such is the ignorance of Nature in large Citys that are
nothing less than overgrown prisons that shut out the
world and all its beautys.

John Clare (1793–1864)
English poet

 Human Nature

Indeed it is remarkable how Nature goes on existing
unofficially, as it were, in the very heart of London.

George Orwell (1903–1950)
English writer

The first sight of green fields with the numberless nodding
gold cups, and the winding river with alders on its banks,
affected me, coming out of a city confinement, with the
sweetness and power of a sudden strain of music.

Samuel Taylor Coleridge (1772–1834)
English poet

Whenever the pressure of our complex city life thins my
blood and benumbs my brain, I seek relief in the trail; and
when I hear the coyote wailing to the yellow dawn, my
cares fall from me—I am happy.

Hamlin Garland (1860–1940)
American novelist

Man and his affairs, church and state and school, trade
and commerce, and manufactures and agriculture, even
politics, the most alarming of them all,—I am pleased to see
how little space they occupy in the landscape.

Henry David Thoreau (1817–1862)
American writer

The peace of the hills is about me and upon me, and the
leisure of the summer clouds, whose shadows I see slowly
drifting across the face of the landscape, is mine. The
dissonance and the turbulence and the stenches of cities—
how far off they seem! the noise and the dust and the
acrimony of politics—how completely the hum of the
honey-bees and the twitter of swallows blot them all out!

John Burroughs (1837–1921)
American writer and naturalist

Among all our good people, not one in a thousand sees the
sun rise once in a year. They know nothing of the morning.
Their idea of it is that it is that part of the day which comes
along after a cup of coffee and a piece of toast.

Daniel Webster (1782–1852)
American statesman and orator

 Human Nature

Now nature, as I am only too well aware, has her
enthusiasts, but on the whole, I am not to be counted
among them. To put it rather bluntly, I am not the type
who wants to go back to the land—I am the type who
wants to go back to the hotel.

Fran Lebowitz (b. 1951)
American humorist

Animals are having a great year, grass was never higher,
flowers were never more in bloom, trees are throwing out
an abundance of shade for us to loaf under. Everything the
Lord has a hand in is going great; but the minute you
notice anything that is in any way under the supervision of
man, why, it's cockeyed.

Will Rogers (1879–1935)
American humorist

Those to whom the trees, the birds, the wildflowers
represent only "locked-up dollars" have never known or
really seen these things.

Edwin Way Teale (1899–1980)
American nature writer

All animals rightly distrust human beings; but when they once feel sure that they do not mean to hurt them, their confidence becomes so great that a man must be worse than a barbarian to abuse it.

Jean-Jacques Rousseau (1712–1778)
Swiss-born French philosopher and writer

The touching appeal of nature, as I have called it therefore, the "Do something kind for me," is not so much a "Live upon me and thrive by me" as "Live *with* me, some-how, and let us make together what we may do for each other—something that is not merely estimable in greasy greenbacks."

Henry James (1843–1916)
American-born writer

240

 Human Nature

Not only the beast but the very elements of Nature seem to rise in revolt against man's dominion. The earth, water, and air become noxious with poisons. Man poisons Nature; Nature poisons man in return: the universal Golden Rule.

John Rodman
20th-century American political scientist

No man finds it difficult to return to nature except the man who has deserted nature.

Seneca (4 B.C.–A.D. 65)
Roman statesman and philosopher

I have asked myself to what extent man's urge to accustom animals to his own way of living is actually an unnatural, or rather an anti-nature, attitude. It seems to me that it is basically symptomatic of man's desire for approval by animals.

Jacques-Yves Cousteau (b. 1910)
French marine explorer

241

"Let us go," we said, "into the Sea of Cortez, realizing that
we become forever a part of it; that our rubber boots
slogging through a flat of eelgrass, that the rocks we turn
over in a tide pool, make us truly and permanently a factor
in the ecology of the region. We shall take something away
from it, but we shall leave something too."

John Steinbeck (1902–1968)
American writer

You yourself, don't you find it a beautiful clean thought, a
world empty of people, just uninterrupted grass, and a hare
sitting up?

D. H. Lawrence (1885–1930)
English novelist and poet

We need the tonic of wildness,—to wade sometimes in
marshes where the bittern and the meadow-hen lurk, and
hear the booming of the snipe; to smell the whispering

 Human Nature

sedge where only some wilder and more solitary fowl
builds her nest, and the mink crawls with its belly close to
the ground.

Henry David Thoreau (1817–1862)
American writer

Long live the weeds and the wilderness yet.

Gerard Manley Hopkins (1844–1889)
English poet and Jesuit priest

Nothing is perfect but primitiveness.

John James Audubon (1785–1851)
American ornithologist

The clearest way into the universe is through a
forest wilderness.

John Muir (1838–1914)
Scottish-born American naturalist

There is not so much virginity in the world that one can afford not to love it when one finds it.

Graham Greene (1904–1991)
English writer

As I watched our gnus posturing, rampant on a field of green grass, I thought how dull the African scene must be now without these gay, frenetic dancers of the veld. It seems that always progress destroys the happy and original, making everything banal, replacing these joyous prancing creatures with the dull, cud-chewing, utilitarian cow.

Gerald Durrell (b. 1925)
English zoologist and writer

Whatever befalls the earth
befalls the sons and daughters of the earth.
We did not weave the web of life;
We are merely a strand in it.
Whatever we do to the web,
we do to ourselves. . . .

Chief Seattle (1788–1866)
Native American (Suquamish) leader

Saving the Planet

Man is not totally compounded of the nature we profess to understand. Man is always partly of the future, and the future he possesses a power to shape.

Loren Eiseley (1907–1977)
American anthropologist

They were all too tightly bound together, men and women, creatures wild and tame, flowers, fruits, and leaves, to ask that any one be spared. As long as the whole continued, the earth could go about its business.

Marjorie Kinnan Rawlings (1896–1953)
American writer

If a man walk in the woods for love of them half of each day, he is in danger of being regarded as a loafer; but if he spends his whole day as a speculator, shearing off those woods and making earth bald before her time, he is esteemed an industrious and enterprising citizen. As if a town had no interest in its forests but to cut them down!

Henry David Thoreau (1817–1862)
American writer

To save what wilderness is left in the American Southwest—
and in the American Southwest only the wilderness is
worth saving—we are going to need all the recruits we
can get.

Edward Abbey (1927–1989)
American writer

We must learn to live more lightly on the land.

Bruce Babbitt (b. 1938)
American politician

When you have seen one ant, one bird, one tree, you have
not seen them all.

Edward O. Wilson (b. 1929)
American entomologist

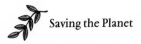 Saving the Planet

Who would kill a rhinoceros? It seems clear that the true aphrodisiac is not found in their horns but in simply knowing they exist.

Terry Tempest Williams (b. 1955)
American nature writer

If a tree dies, plant another in its place.

Linnaeus (1707–1778)
Swedish botanist

Though boys throw stones at frogs in sport, the frogs do not die in sport, but in earnest.

Bion (c. 280 B.C.)
Greek poet

Wilderness is a resource which can shrink but not grow. . . .
the creation of new wilderness in the full sense of the word
is impossible.

Aldo Leopold (1888–1948)
American conservationist and writer

Nature is neutral. Man has wrested from nature the power
to make the world a desert or to make the deserts bloom.
There is no evil in the atom; only in men's souls.

Adlai Stevenson (1900–1965)
American politician

Oxygen is not a major worry for us, unless we let fly with
enough nuclear explosives to kill off the green cells in the
sea; if we do that, of course, we are in for strangling.

Lewis Thomas (b. 1913)
American physician and writer

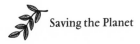 Saving the Planet

... And He said: This is a beautiful world that I have given
   you.
Take good care of it; do not ruin it.

Jewish prayer

From Nature's chain whatever link you strike,
Tenth, or ten thousandth, breaks the chain alike.

Alexander Pope (1868–1744)
English poet

It means nothing to strike up a friendship with a sea lion or a dolphin if, at the same time, we are destroying their last refuges along our coasts and our islands. It is an exercise in vanity and absurdity to try to communicate with a killer whale and then to put it on exhibition in an aquatic zoo as a circus freak.

Jacques-Yves Cousteau (b. 1910)
French marine explorer

God hath not taken all that pains in forming, framing, furnishing, and adorning this world, that they who were made by him to live in it, should despise it.

Edward Hyde, Earl of Clarendon (1609–1674)
English historian and statesman

Now she has risen into sight, our one familiar moon. A beautiful world to our eyes, but cold and lifeless; without

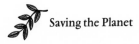

water or atmosphere she is a presage of what Earth
might become.

Jacquetta Hawkes (b. 1910)
English archaeologist and writer

We may be able to survive in a world where the giant
panda, the California condor and the black rhino exist
only as pictures in a book. But do we want to?

Jack Hanna (b. 1947)
American zoo director

The rains bring us trees and flowers; the droughts bring
gaping cracks in the world. The lakes and rivers sustain us;
they flow through the veins of the earth and into our own.
But we must take care to let them flow back out as pure as
they came, not poison and waste them without thought for
the future.

Al Gore (b. 1948)
American politician

251

The cult of wilderness is not a luxury; it is a necessity
for the protection of humanized nature and for the
preservation of mental health.

Rene Dubos (1901–1982)
French microbiologist and environmentalist

Hurt not the earth—neither the sea—nor the trees.

Revelations 7:3

The swan song sounded by the wilderness grows fainter,
ever more constricted, until only sharp ears can catch it at
all. It fades to a nearly inaudible level, and yet there never is
going to be any one time when we can say right now it
is gone.

Edward Hoagland (b. 1932)
American writer

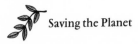 Saving the Planet

Teach your children
what we have taught our children —
that the earth is our mother.
Whatever befalls the earth
befalls the sons and daughters of the earth.

Chief Seattle (1788–1866)
Native American (Suquamish) leader

Earth has no sorrows that earth cannot heal.

John Muir (1838–1914)
Scottish-born American naturalist

In Harmony with Nature

I know that the whicker of a plover in the September sky doesn't touch all other men in their bowels as it touches me, and that men whom it doesn't touch at all can be good men. But it touches me. And I care about knowing what it is, and—if I can—why.

John Graves (b. 1920)
American nature writer

The Kikuyus, when left to themselves, do not bury their dead, but leave them above ground for the Hyenas and vultures to deal with. The custom had always appealed to me. I thought that it would be a pleasant thing to be laid out to the sun and stars, and to be so promptly, neatly and openly picked and cleansed; to be made one with Nature and become a common component of a landscape.

Isak Dinesen (Karen Blixen, 1885–1962)
Danish writer

 In Harmony with Nature

All that is harmony for thee, O Universe, is in harmony
with me as well. Nothing that comes at the right time for
thee is too early or too late for me. Everything is fruit to me
that thy seasons bring, O Nature. All things come of thee,
have their being in thee, and return to thee.

Marcus Aurelius (121–180 A.D.)
Roman emperor and philosopher

There is not a sprig of grass that shoots uninteresting to
me, nor any thing that moves.

Thomas Jefferson (1743–1826)
American statesman

Now, when there are billions of people, and not so many
trees, it is sustaining to imagine what it might be like to
open one's flowers on a spring afternoon, or to stand
silently, making food out of sunlight, for a thousand years.
It gives proportion to the world.

David Rains Wallace (b. 1945)
American writer

The goal of life is living in agreement with Nature.

Zeno (335–263 B.C.)
Greek Stoic philosopher

My idea of gardening is to discover something wild in my
wood and weed around it with the utmost care until it has a
chance to grow and spread.

Margaret Bourke-White (1906–1971)
American photographer

I don't know whether a passionate love of the natural
world can be transmitted or not, but like the love of
beauty it is a thing one likes to associate with the scheme
of inheritance.

E. B. White (1899–1985)
American writer

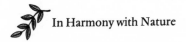

Shall I not have intelligence with the earth? Am I not partly leaves and vegetable mould myself?

Henry David Thoreau (1817–1862)
American writer

At home one should see and hear with more fondness and sympathy. Nature should touch him a little more closely there than anywhere else. He is better attuned to it than to strange scenes. The birds about his own door are his birds, the flowers in his own fields and wood are his, the rainbow springs its magic arch across his valley, even the everlasting stars to which one lifts his eye, night after night, and year after year, from his own doorstep, have something private and personal about them.

John Burroughs (1837–1921)
American writer and naturalist

257

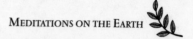

Once in his life a man ought to concentrate his mind upon the remembered earth. He ought to give himself up to a particular landscape in his experience; to look at it from as many angles as he can, to wonder upon it, to dwell upon it.

N. Scott Momaday (b. 1934)
American writer

I feel the centipede in me,—cayman, carp, eagle, and fox. I am moved by strange sympathies; I say continually "I will be a naturalist."

Ralph Waldo Emerson (1803–1882)
American poet and essayist

I do not know whether I was then a man dreaming I was a butterfly, or whether I am now a butterfly dreaming I am a man.

Chuang Tzu (369–286 B.C.)
Chinese sage

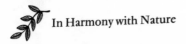

For the first time in my life the weather was not something
that touched me, that caressed me, froze or sweated me,
but became me. The atmosphere and I became the same.
Soft infinitesimal showers of microscopic bugs fanned
down on my face as I slept, and they were extremely
pleasant and soothing.

Jack Kerouac (1922–1969)
American writer

I am a part of all you see
In Nature: part of all you feel:
I am the impact of the bee
Upon the blossom; in the tree
I am the sap—that shall reveal
The leaf, the bloom—that flows and flutes
Up from the darkness through its roots.

Madison Cawein (1865–1914)
American poet

Which of us is not sometimes affected, almost to despair,
by the splendid vision of earth and sky?

John Keble (1795–1812)
English clergyman

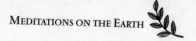

I am at two with nature.

Woody Allen (b. 1935)
American film director, writer, and actor

You can grow intimate with almost any living thing,
transfer to it your own emotion of tenderness, nostalgia,
regret, so that often of a relationship one remembers the
scene with the most affection. A particular line of hedge in
a Midland county, a drift of leaves in a particular wood: it is
only human to imagine that we receive back from these the
feeling someone left with them.

Graham Greene (1904–1991)
English writer

I live not in myself, but I become
Portion of that around me: and to me
High mountains are a feeling, but the hum
Of human cities torture.

George Gordon, Lord Byron (1788–1824)
English poet

 In Harmony with Nature

We are the offspring of history, and must establish our own paths in this most diverse and interesting of conceivable universes—one indifferent to our suffering, and therefore offering us maximal freedom to thrive, or to fail, in our own chosen way.

Stephen Jay Gould (b. 1941)
Biologist and historian

Let us a little permit Nature to take her own way; she better understands her own affairs than we.

Michel Eyquem de Montaigne (1533–1592)
French essayist

A Sense of Wonder

I always think that this month the prophet of spring brings
many beautys to the landscape tho a careless observer
would laugh at me for saying so who believes that it brings
nothing because he does not give himself the trouble to
seek them . . .

John Clare (1793–1864)
English poet

If I were a painter, I would go to nature for all my patterns.

Thomas Bewick (1753–1828)
English illustrator and engraver

In beauty, I walk
To the direction of the rising sun
In beauty, I walk
To the direction traveling with the sun
In beauty, I walk

 A Sense of Wonder

To the direction of the setting sun
In beauty, I walk. . .
All around me my land is beauty
In beauty, I walk

Navajo (Yebechei) chant

Lord make us mindful of the little things that grow and
blossom in these days to make the world beautiful for us.

W. E. B. DuBois (1868–1963)
American writer and educator

"Creeping" and "flying" are established in our vocabulary
as the very symbols of the most contemptible and the most
glorious forms of motion. Yet the caterpillar who went to
sleep ignorant of anything except creeping wakes up to
waft himself nonchalantly away on the most beautiful
wings either nature or the human imagination has ever
been able to imagine.

Joseph Wood Krutch (1893–1970)
American writer

... I knew the birds
and insects, which looked fathered by the flowers ...
    butterflies, that bear
Upon their blue wings such red embers round
They seem to scorch the blue air into holes
Each flight they take ...

Elizabeth Barrett Browning (1806–1861)
English poet

But the cliffs were no longe white. They burned now with
the deep red sunset glow of the desert, the glow that catches
your breath and quietens the striving and makes you want
to manacle time so that the beauty can go on and on.

Colin Fletcher (b. 1922)
Welsh hiker and writer

It is a beautiful and a blessed world we live in, and while life
lasts, to lose the enjoyment of it is a sin.

Talbot Wilson Chambers (1819–1896)
American clergyman

264

 A Sense of Wonder

In my room, my prayers are not so frequent or so fervent;
but, at the sight of a beautiful landscape, I feel myself
moved without knowing why.

Jean-Jacques Rousseau (1712–1778)
Swiss-born French philosopher and writer

If beautiful objects had been created solely for man's
gratification, it ought to be shown that before man
appeared, there was less beauty on the face of the earth
than since he came on the stage. Were the beautiful volute
and cone shells of the Eocene epoch, and the gracefully
sculptured ammonite of the Secondary period, created
that man might ages afterward admire them in his cabinet?

Charles Darwin (1809–1882)
English naturalist and scientist

Remember that the most beautiful things in the world are
the most useless; peacocks and lilies for instance.

John Ruskin (1819–1900)
English critic and essayist

... there is indeed a chasm which separates man and animal, and ... if that chasm is to be bridged, it must be man who does it by means of understanding. But before we can understand, we must know; and to know, we must love. We must love life in all its forms, even in those which we find least attractive.

Jacques-Yves Cousteau (b. 1910)
French marine explorer

Lilies that fester smell far worse than weeds.

William Shakespeare (1564–1616)
English playwright and poet

I wanted to say something about the universe. There's God, angels, plants ... and horseshit.

Zero Mostel (1915–1977)
American actor

Nature does have manure and she does have roots as well as blossoms, and you can't hate the manure and blame the roots for not being blossoms.

Buckminster Fuller (1895–1983)
American engineer and philosopher

BRICK: Well, they say nature abhors a vacuum, Big Daddy.
BIG DADDY: That's what they say, but sometimes I think that a vacuum is a hell of a lot better than some of the stuff that nature replaces it with.

Tennessee Williams (1911–1983)
American playwright

With minute and amateurish interest, I found atop a scoop in the base of a big, drifted, scorched tree trunk five little piles of fox dung, a big owl's puke ball full of hair and rat skulls, and three fresher piles of what had to be coon droppings . . . . Why, intrigued ignorance asked, did wild things so often choose to stool on rocks, stumps, and other elevations?

Commonsense replied: Maybe for the view.

John Graves (b. 1920)
American nature writer

Nature is pleased with simplicity, and affects not the pomp
of superfluous causes.

Isaac Newton (1642–1727)
English physicist

In all things of nature there is
something of the marvelous.

Aristotle (384–322 B.C.)
Greek philosopher

Nature speaks in symbols
and in signs.

John Greenleaf Whittier (1807–1892)
American poet

268

The untaught peasant beheld the elements around him, and was acquainted with their practical uses. The most learned philosopher knew little more. He had partially unveiled the face of Nature, but her immortal lineaments were still a wonder and a mystery. He might anatomise, and give names; but, not to speak of a final cause, causes in their secondary and tertiary grades were utterly unknown to him.

Mary Wollstonecraft Shelley (1797–1851)
English novelist

We understand nature just as if, at a distance, we looked at the image of a person in a looking-glass, plainly and fervently discoursing, yet what he uttered we could decipher only by the motion of the lips or by his mien.

Samuel Taylor Coleridge (1772–1834)
English poet

The earth is rude, silent, incomprehensible at first, Nature
is rude and incomprehensible at first,
Be not discouraged, keep on, there are divine
things well envelop'd,
I swear to you there are divine things more beautiful than
words can tell.

Walt Whitman (1819–1892)
American poet

Nature is wont to hide herself.

Heraclitus (c. 540–c. 480 B.C.)
Greek philosopher

I have never asked that nature open any doors to reveal the
truth of spirit or mystery; I aspire to no shaman's path; I
expect no vision, no miracles except the ones that fill every
instant of ordinary life.

Richard K. Nelson (b. 1941)
American anthropologist

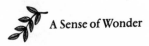 A Sense of Wonder

Late on the third day, at the very moment when, at
sunset, we were making our way through a herd of
hippopotamuses, there flashed upon my mind, unforeseen
and unsought, the phrase, "Reverence for life."

Albert Schweitzer (1875–1965)
French philosopher, clergyman, and medical missionary

. . . [Nature] is the one place where miracles not only
happen, but happen all the time.

Thomas Wolfe (1900–1938)
American novelist

It is an outcome of faith that nature—as she is perceptible
to our five senses—takes the character of such a well-
formulated puzzle.

Albert Einstein (1879—1955)
German-born American physicist

Tiny white crystalline flakes falling through the air, billions of them which when you take some in your hand and study them, no two are the same. You can't study them long because they melt in your hand, but no two are the same, that's what they say. But who said this? Who would do a study of billions of snowflakes to prove no repetition?

Garrison Keillor (b. 1942)
American humorist

Nature is an infinite sphere of which the centre is everywhere, and the circumference nowhere.

Blaise Pascal (1623–1662)
French scientist and philosopher

Unknown to me what resideth here
Tears flow from a sense of unworthiness and gratitude.

Anonymous Japanese poet

One vivid memory remains of passing through the city.
A small boy, five or six at most, had picked up a dead
monarch butterfly from a pile of litter beside the street. He
was standing entranced, bending forward, oblivious to all
around him. It seemed as though I were looking at myself
when young. A door was opening for him, a door beyond
which lay all the beauty and mystery of nature.

Edwin Way Teale (1899–1980)
American nature writer

Worlds can be found by a child and an adult bending
down and looking together under the grass stems or at the
skittering crabs in a tidal pool.

Mary Catherine Bateson (b. 1939)
American anthropologist

There is no enough in Nature. It is one vast prodigality. It is
a feast.

Richard Jefferies (1848–1887)
English writer

Spring's immortality was in us; ever-living earth was better than any home in the stars which eye hath not seen nor heart conceived. Nature was all in all; we worshipped her and her wordless messages in our heart were sweeter than honey and the honeycomb.

W. H. Hudson (1841–1922)
Argentine-born English writer

We see as fine risings of the sun as ever Adam saw; and its risings are as much a miracle now as they were in his day— and, I think, a good deal more, because it is now part of the miracle, that for thousands and thousands of years he has come to his appointed time, without the variation of a millionth part of a second.

Daniel Webster (1782–1852)
American statesman and orator

There is religion in everything around us,
A calm and holy religion
In the unbreathing things in Nature.

John Ruskin (1819–1900)
English critic and essayist

274

The country is both the philosopher's garden and his library, in which he reads and contemplates the power, wisdom, and goodness of God.

William Penn (1644–1718)
English religious reformer and colonialist

The day does not seem wholly profane in which we have given heed to some natural object.

Ralph Waldo Emerson (1803–1882)
American essayist and poet

Here, man is no longer the center of the world, only a witness, but a witness who is also a partner in the silent life of nature, bound by secret affinities to the trees.

Dag Hammarskjöld (1905–1961)
Swedish diplomat and humanitarian

He prayeth well, who loveth well
Both man and bird and beast.

Samuel Taylor Coleridge (1772–1834)
English poet

If we do not go to church as much as did our fathers, we go
to the woods much more, and are much more inclined to
make a temple of them than they were.

John Burroughs (1837–1921)
American writer and naturalist

In the beginning of all things, wisdom and knowledge were
with the animals, for Tirawa, the One Above, did not speak
directly to man. He sent certain animals to tell men that he
showed himself through the beasts, and that from them,
and from the stars and the sun and the moon should
man learn.

Eagle Chief (Letakots-Lesa)
19th-century Native American (Pawnee)

 A Sense of Wonder

The creator created the Earth, our Mother Earth, and gave
her many duties, among them to care for us, His people.
He put things upon Mother Earth for the benefit of all.
And as we travel around today we see that our Mother
Earth is still doing her duty, and that we are very grateful.

Irving Powless, Sr.
20th-century Native American (Onondaga) chief

I have a strange longing for the great simple primeval
things, such as the sea, to me no less of a mother than
the Earth.

Oscar Wilde (1854–1900)
Irish playwright, poet, and writer

Thus weave for us a garment of brightness
That we may walk fittingly where grass is green,
O our mother the earth, O our father the sky!

Tewa Pueblo prayer

Among the scenes which are deeply impressed on my mind, none exceed in sublimity the primeval forests undefaced by the hand of man; whether those of Brazil, where the powers of Life are predominant, or those of Tiera del Fuego, where Death and Decay prevail. Both are temples filled with the varied productions of the God of Nature:—no one can stand in these solitudes unmoved, and not feel that there is more in man than the mere breath of his body.

Charles Darwin (1809–1882)
English naturalist and scientist

The book of nature is like a page written over or printed upon with different-sized characters and in many different languages, interlined and crosslined, and with a great variety of marginal notes and references. There is coarse print and fine print; there are obscure signs and hieroglyphics. . . . It is a book which he reads best who goes most slowly or even tarries long by the way.

John Burroughs (1837–1921)
American writer and naturalist

278

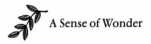

For we are no longer isolated, standing like starry visitors on a mountain-top, surveying life from the outside; but are on a level with and part and parcel of it; and if the mystery of life daily deepens, it is because we view it more closely and with clearer vision.

W. H. Hudson (1841–1922)
Argentine-born English writer

Index of Names

Index

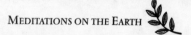

Index

Index

Index